NEW AGE TO JESUS

Ten True Stories of Redemption

Lucinda Button

Sarah Grace
Publishing
Dyslexic Friendly

Cover design by Esther Kotecha
Art direction by Sarah Grace

Printed in the UK

The creation of this book was only made possible because of the authors' willingness to share their often raw and deeply personal testimonies. Thank you all. Without God there would be no testimonies to share, so all glory goes to Him.

'And they have conquered him
by the blood of the Lamb and by
the word of their testimony'
Revelation 12:11.

Jenny Horner
Candice-Marie Machajewski
Charlotte Meadows
Jonathan Golby
Amber Louise Reif
Kate Orson
Jackie Harris
Katerina Hasapopoulos
Laura Maxwell

Contents

Endorsements

"In these thrilling escape stories, we have ten accounts of people who were trapped in the darkest depths of various New Age practices but who have found rescue, freedom and true peace in Jesus Christ! A book that deserves the widest circulation."

J.John, Evangelist

"I can't remember the last time I felt so excited about a book. Yet this is far more than just a book — it's a lifeline for those caught in the snare of New Age deception. God is moving powerfully among those trapped in the New Age, opening eyes and bringing true freedom through the only Light that can save — Jesus Christ.

The enemy always counterfeits God's truth and the gifts of His Spirit, seeking to keep people bound in darkness and false hope. But the gospel still breaks chains, rescues hearts, and transforms lives.

New Age to Jesus will not only inspire you, but also equip you with understanding. Most of all, it will remind you that the gospel of Jesus Christ is still the power of God unto salvation. Light will always triumph over darkness — and this book shows you ten unforgettable examples."

Rod Williams, Evangelist and Author of *The Real Deal*

"Raw, visceral, highly informative, heart-wrenching, at times disturbing, always ultimately redemptive and glorious, this collection of personal life stories is essential reading for a generation spiritually hungry for the truth – I couldn't put it down."

Dominic Muir
Founder, David's Tent, Bread Cafe, National co-leader of King's Army UK

"This book is a powerful testimony to the relentless love of Jesus Christ.

More than that this book will show readers that Jesus is very much alive today!

In these ten true stories, you'll witness people stepping out of the deceptive glow of the New Age into the life-giving light of the Gospel.

Each account is raw, honest, and deeply moving, showing not only the emptiness of false spirituality but also the fullness and freedom found in Christ.

As someone who understands the pull of spiritual counterfeits and the miraculous power of His grace, I was deeply stirred reading these pages.

This is not just a book of testimonies – it's a reminder that no one is too far gone for the saving hand of Jesus, and that His truth still sets captives free. I believe these stories will inspire, convict, and ignite hope in every reader."

Riaan Swiegelaar
Cape Town, SA

Foreword

Stories are powerful.

I was speaking from a rickety stage to a tightly-packed crowd of several thousand people in a field. A lady called Theresa was listening about a stone's throw away, maybe thirty yards out. Her life was a mess, and she was plagued with evil spirits. On that day, they had told her to go to the open-air meeting and wait until the speaker reached the climax of his message. When he got to the point of Jesus' death and resurrection, she was to cause as big a disturbance as possible to interrupt people's response when the speaker invited the audience to surrender their lives to Him.

Of course, I knew none of this, but as I spoke of Jesus' invitation to new life through His death on a cross, suddenly there was a commotion and I saw a flip-flop flung at me. It sailed past me on my right, and a few seconds later another one sailed past my left. There was a tussle in front of me and the crowd parted as four men carried this writhing lady backstage. All of this was caught on camera.

We concluded the meeting. Many people responded to God's offer of forgiveness and freedom in Christ. Indeed, one of the people who received total freedom was Theresa herself. As she was prayed over, the demons were identified and cast out in the name of Jesus. We filmed her a few days later, and she shared how the demons within her had said at that moment: 'Right, now's the time, disrupt the meeting!' She now had a glorious carefree smile on her face. She'd not slept properly in years as she was riddled with fear and tormented by those spirits, but she'd just enjoyed three nights in a row of peaceful sleep for the first time.

Both the flip-flop-throwing and the interview are on film as evidence. I say that, because it is legitimate to query any story as to whether it actually happened. But if it's true, it's really powerful, it's undeniable, and it demands a response.

What you have in this important book are ten life stories that are true. They might sound a little crazy – like the one above – and all the more so, if you have had no experience of New Age teachings and practices. But if you read them with an open mind, I believe they will really help in challenging your worldview. There is so much more going on than meets the eye.

On the other hand, if you are familiar with New Age practices and are seeking after truth, the common thread through all these stories is that the quest for truth culminated in a life-transforming encounter that brought healing, freedom and restoration. Who wouldn't want that?! So however challenging to your thinking, keep reading until the very end.

The Truth will set you free!

Simon Guillebaud
Great Lakes Outreach

Introduction

This book is a collection of ten testimonies. They are the personal stories of people who were seeking spiritual truth in many different places, who all found that the ultimate peace and joy is found in Jesus. All the contributors to this book are members of The Bridge, which started as a Facebook group, and is made up of followers of Jesus and seekers of truth. The bridge is a ministry that supports people across the bridge from new age spirituality into a life believing in Jesus, and I set it up after I had just taken that very journey. I wanted to expose the deception of New Age spirituality and help people find their way out, as I had done.

You may have this book in your hands as a seeker of truth yourself, and although you've been diligently pursuing spiritual practices, you still haven't found the consistent contentment you've been reaching for. My hope is that these stories will inspire you and help to lead you home.

Or maybe you are a long-term Christian with little to no experience of the New Age, in which case you will find encouragement and information in these pages. You will learn how and why people end up in the New Age and what they need in terms of support.

Over the past decade New Age spirituality has become mainstream. You can walk into most major high street retailers and easily find products such as 'spell' colouring books for children, Tarot cards or tote bags decorated with satanic symbology – and this is just the tip of the iceberg. Nowadays the New Age is often the first place people go when they are in need of physical or emotional healing; the New Age could now be seen as the spiritual zeitgeist.

Apart from Laura's story all these testimonies have taken place over the last few years, and all the writers are from the UK except Amber who is in the US.

Each contributor realised that they were not only deceived but that they were separated from God. They discovered that faith in Jesus and his death and resurrection was the truth they had been seeking, and that through *faith* they would find *forgiveness* and *freedom*.

> 'For it is by grace you have been saved, through faith.' (Ephesians 2:8)

> 'For God so loved the world that he gave his one and only Son, that whoever believes in him shall not perish but have eternal life.' (John 3:16)

Whoever you are and whatever the reason you have this book in your hands right now, my prayer is that it will bless you.

Love, Lucinda
Founder of The Bridge Ministry

Jenny's Story

My childhood was a bit unstable. I grew up in a small, rough town in England. We didn't have much money and my parents divorced when I was a kid. I couldn't speak at primary school and had no friends. My mum and dad were both struggling with their own issues, so they weren't able to help me with mine. Growing up with a mum with mental illness meant that she was a bit emotionally distant, even though I was always well looked after.

My parents were both atheists, and I was taught evolution at school, so I didn't believe in God. I would often sit and think about death; I imagined existing all by myself in a white room of nothingness somewhere, forever trapped with no one to talk to. It was a scary thought. Or perhaps we just stopped existing altogether. That was an even scarier thought. What scared me the most, though, was dying young without having lived my life to the full, whatever that meant. I definitely didn't believe in heaven or hell. That was just in cartoons, wasn't it?

Teenage Troubles

When I was in my teens, I discovered that the spirit realm was real after playing with a homemade Ouija board with friends. I thought that I had spoken to my dead grandad.

'Where's Grandma?' I asked.

'*In bed,*' it responded, before the planchette flew back and forth between the number six, three times.

Ever since that day, I thought that my grandma and grandad were tucked up in bed in the afterlife. I also had a lot of fear from other supernatural events that had happened to me, and also to my relatives who were involved in Spiritualism. They had been troubled by a poltergeist that appeared as an old man and tormented their child. They moved house eventually, but it followed them. It was typical horror-movie stuff, like seeing shadows, hearing footsteps, and objects flying off the shelves in the kitchen.

Like many teenagers, I didn't know what I was supposed to be doing with my life and was just following the crowd. Listening to mainstream music made me think that sin was normal, like having sex before marriage and partying. By the time I was fourteen, I was caught up in the rave scene, and going clubbing around the UK. I was getting into fights, taking party drugs, going to illegal raves and doing other dangerous things like drink driving. Sometimes I would drink until I blacked out and wouldn't remember a thing. I just thought it was normal because the people around me were doing similar things, including my dad and my sister. I was also self-medicating with recreational drugs and alcohol to help the undiagnosed social anxiety I was struggling with. I didn't understand why I couldn't talk to people unless I was high or drunk. My mum always told me I'd grow out of my shyness, as she called it, but it only got worse. Eventually, she kicked me out when I was sixteen because I was getting out of control.

I didn't have much self-confidence. I was also bullied at school for having speech problems and buck teeth, and for being 'stupid' and 'skinny'. When I smiled people would laugh at my teeth. I never felt confident in the way I looked, the way I spoke, or in my abilities. It seemed like the only thing I was any good at was partying and rolling cigarettes.

I went to university and tried to become successful, but my social anxiety always got in the way, so I continued self-medicating. I went festival hopping around Europe, moved to Ibiza for the season and flew to Burning Man Festival alone, where I ended up staying at a 'polyamorous' campsite. The life I was living looked glamorous; hanging out with famous DJs, getting free entry into famous nightclubs and drinking champagne every day. On the outside, I looked like I had a great life, but I was always overdosing on drugs and was surrounded by people who didn't care about me. Deep down, I wanted a healthy life of stability but I didn't know how. I thought there was something wrong with me – that I was somehow broken.

Enticed into the Occult

When I was in Ibiza, I was introduced to a book called *The Secret* by Rhonda Byrne, which was about 'manifestation'. After reading the book, I visualised myself holding a €50 note. Just a few hours later, a man came up to me in the street and handed me a €50 note as I was standing at a bus stop.

'Get a taxi,' he said.

Wow! *The Secret* was real. I started to think my thoughts were creating my reality and that I was in control. What didn't occur to me, was that I was actually practising a form of witchcraft and I was really only manifesting demons into my life. I was seemingly able to manifest things at rapid speed and even altered the grade of my university degree from a 2:2 to a 2:1, after the final marks were in. It didn't take long to fall down into the New Age rabbit hole, where I read many self-help books to try and improve myself. I also started practising meditation to get rid of my negative thoughts, so that I would have more control over my reality. I loved the peace and euphoria it gave me. Sometimes, I would meditate for hours on end. It was my new addiction; meditating came very easily to me. I would sit down to meditate and, after just a few moments, my body would start to rock backwards and forwards and then in a circular motion before entering into a trance. I just thought it was normal.

One day, whilst meditating, I felt a spirit enter my body. It felt like a large ball of fire, which came shooting up through the floor and into my head. I jolted out of the trance.

'What on earth was that?' I said to myself.

That was the end of my obsession with meditation. I was terrified.

After that happened, things went from bad to worse and I ended up living a very reckless lifestyle. I was sugar-dating, dancing in exotic clubs and putting myself in very dangerous situations, hoping I would die. I even lived rough on the streets on occasion, drinking very strong alcohol. After some time, I had an epiphany and decided to find a rich man to support me so I could get sober.

The False Light Deception

It was now five years after the spirit had entered my body during meditation. On the surface it looked like I had turned my life around, as I was now living a flashy lifestyle by the beach. Jet-setting to my bucket-list destinations with a brain surgeon and running around Tokyo and America on shopping sprees. My life revolved around eating at five-star restaurants, going to the gym and attending hair and beauty appointments. I was totally obsessed with my appearance and fixing myself. Out of the blue, I was awoken in the middle of the night by a voice.

'Go for a walk,' it said. I shot bolt upright in bed and looked at the clock. It was early in the morning at around 3am.

'Was that the voice of God?' I said to myself.

I had no idea who or even what God was at the time, but I had a gut feeling that something big was about to happen that day. I climbed up to the top of a cliff edge and sat waiting for the sunrise. When I turned around to go back home, I almost fell over ... everything looked completely different. I felt like I was seeing the world for the very first time. A veil had been lifted and I was able to see into the spiritual realm.

My mind was totally void of thoughts and I saw that there was a formless intelligence, or spirit, inside of me. I started to receive supernatural downloads, which came directly into my spirit, rather than into my mind as thoughts. This is very hard to describe and put into words but I will try.

'The person you always thought you were was an illusion created by your thoughts. The spirit inside of you is the real you. You are God. Separateness is an illusion. All is one. Time is an illusion.' I turned around and looked at the rocks and plants and everything looked alive. I felt like I had just woken up from a really bad dream and had suddenly got the punchline of a big cosmic joke which I'd been playing on myself all along. It was all just a big magic trick. I was God in a meat suit, and so was everyone else. They just hadn't realised it yet.

I later came to discover that what had happened to me was what people called 'self-realisation'. What I didn't know was that I was actually the punchline of a much more sinister joke being played on me – that I had been initiated into the greatest demonic deception of all time, known as 'spiritual enlightenment'. I felt like I had been re-born, but I had actually just been born into the false light.

I walked around for many months staring at everything in amazement. Everything was so bright, colourful and ... 5D? I felt like Alice in Wonderland. It was completely different to the old grey world that I was used to. Everything was magical and exciting. It was during this time that I started to have mystical visions. One day, whilst walking through the city, my consciousness expanded up into the sky and I felt like I was looking down on the city from a bird's eye view.

The spirit in me spoke again.

'There is only really one character here, playing all of the different parts in this game of life. They have forgotten who they are.'

I was even given a vision of my so-called past life. In the vision, the spirit showed me that I was a black man from America and that my wife had killed us in a car crash. I saw his whole life like a movie being played backwards, before seeing myself being born in the hospital. After this, I believed in reincarnation and thought that I had lived thousands of lives. I also noticed that I had psychic abilities; I knew things about people I had no way of knowing ordinarily. I could see through objects after meditating and I could also see auras and energy, including a large energetic grid made of geometry.

I wanted to know more about what had happened to me and so I started reading spiritual books. I lost interest in the worldly things I had been doing beforehand, like partying, and I became fascinated with the occult. I read many, many books from all different kinds of spiritual teachers. I studied many metaphysical topics and I thought I was some kind of mystic, on a mission to help the planet awaken to their so-called divinity. I even ended up on some paranormal investigations at a haunted jail.

To my amazement, everything that the spirit had taught me in visions and downloads was being taught by these well-known spiritual teachers and Eastern religions. The Hindus called the illusion 'Maya'. It seemed like all religions were talking about the same God, but in slightly different ways. I felt sorry for Christians. I thought they had been brainwashed by a dusty old book and had not realised that Jesus was trying to tell us that we were God ... or was he?

I had never read the Bible, but all of my favourite spiritual teachers quoted from it, so I became familiar with a lot of popular Bible verses such as 'the kingdom of heaven is within'. However, these verses were taken out of context, so I didn't really know what Jesus was teaching at all.

I also went to yoga school and became a Reiki and Pellowah healer. I was told by the teachers that I had a gift of connecting with energy. What I wasn't told was that the attunement ceremonies were actually occult initiations and that through them I had entered into a covenant with demons. I'd made an agreement to receive counterfeit healing powers under the guise of 'energy healing'. I thought I was healing people when what I was actually doing was transferring unclean spirits into them!

Although I thought I was 'enlightened', I was still living a sinful life as I believed evil was just an illusion. I was polyamorous and bisexual, I was fornicating, lying, practising witchcraft and committing many more sins. I thought marriage was a manmade construct, not from God, and I couldn't see myself having kids because my life was so unstable.

At one point I received a prophecy from a Chi Master. He told me I was going to be a facilitator of change, along with many things about myself which were true – so naturally I believed him. It felt like my 'spirit guides' were preparing me for something big. The Chi Master said I was going to help change society, and after a long series of events and a near-death experience, which I won't go into here, I channelled a book about 'Christ consciousness', which I believed was coming from God.

The way it happened was that at the same time every morning, the spirit woke me up to write. The words just flowed out of me automatically. The book was talking about many spiritual concepts, which at that point I had never heard of before. I actually thought I was unlocking the secrets of the universe. It was even talking about Christian concepts such as the Trinity, but in a new context. The book was called *The Spider and the Cosmic Illusion*.

After the first draft of the book was complete, I took a few days off and went outside for a walk, only to find a box of brand-new books on the floor in the street. I picked up a copy.

'Have you finished your first draft?' it read.

Wow! A book about how to edit your book. Nothing seemed to surprise me anymore. I felt guided, protected, loved and supported by the universe, God and angels. I knew that the book was going to make a lot of money, because it was backed by the spiritual realm. What I didn't realise was that I was channelling from demons.

I decided that I would spend the profits on building accommodation for the homeless, where they would not be indoctrinated into Christianity. I was disappointed that the majority of homeless shelters in my area seemed to be run by Christian organisations. The spirit was leading me to support the homeless, whilst initiating them into meditation, yoga and the New Age deception.

Kundalini Awakening aka Full Demonic Possession

I was on the final edit of the book when I started to get a burning pain in my stomach, above my belly button. It felt like a strange fire burning away at something. I was also burping throughout the day, and it felt like I was being pulled out of my body at random times. The doctors didn't know what was wrong with me and thought I had gastritis, but the medication was not working.

One day, when I was walking back to my apartment, I went into a spontaneous trance. The spirit had fully taken over. I was possessed. What was happening? I panicked as I could not return to my ordinary state of consciousness and started calling on the spirit for help. The word *portal* jumped out at me, which was written in large letters on a road sign near my apartment. I had walked past it many times, but had never seen it before. Had I opened a portal? Things were getting stranger than ever before. What happened next was so terrifying that it cannot be put into words.

As I sat at my desk on my laptop trying to find help, my body started to move around in a circle, just like it did when I meditated. Then, suddenly, I felt something in my stomach pop, and what felt like ten thousand volts of electricity rushed up to my head and started to fry my brain. I ran to the toilet, where I proceeded to projectile vomit and have green diarrhoea.

After around two weeks, I realised I was having a spontaneous 'Kundalini awakening'. In the New Age the 'Kundalini' is said to be a divine dormant energy at the base of the spine, which leads to spiritual enlightenment once activated through yoga and meditation. I was not trying to have a 'Kundalini awakening', and I had actually always avoided the Kundalini form of yoga. However, I had done hundreds, if not thousands, of hours of meditation and other occult practices over the years. At the time that this happened, I was sleeping on my yoga mat with no pillow and waking up at 4am to do meditation and yoga, before chanting Hindu mantras, drawing Pellowah symbols and doing other New Age practices until 7am.

Over the next three months I was violently electrocuted every day by an unknown force. I was constantly squeezing my head, which felt like a balloon that was about to pop. I had insomnia and could not regulate my body temperature. I could hardly see properly anymore and felt like a giant. Everything was so distorted and bright and I could see 'energy' everywhere. I had to wear sunglasses for three months, even indoors. At other times, the spirit would start electrocuting me. I had to lie down for hours until the shaking and heart palpitations had stopped. Sometimes, I had to run around, frantically trying to get rid of some of the energy because I felt like I was going to explode.

I was no longer able to hold water down as I would vomit whenever I drank or ate anything. I was no longer able to sleep as I had too much energy and kept having visions when I closed my eyes. I came to realise that this unknown 'force' was intelligent. It had a mind of its own. It was a person without a body. When I did certain things that it didn't want me to do, such as going on my laptop to find help, it would move up to my head again and fry my brain. Around one-third to a half of my hair fell out and my two big toenails fell off!

I started to think I would die of a heart attack, dehydration or something else. I wished I had never started meditating that day in my bedroom at university almost ten years prior. This wasn't what I had signed up for. I had only been seeking truth and healing. The spirit seemed evil and didn't care about my welfare. At times, I felt like I was the luckiest person on earth, and at other times, I questioned the nature of this spirit. If it was divine, why did it seem so evil? I feared that if it didn't kill me, I would never be able to live a normal life again.

I knew that the hospital wouldn't be able to do anything for me. You can go to the hospital with a broken leg, but what about a spirit that's wreaking havoc on your body and mind? I knew they wouldn't understand my situation and I didn't want to get sectioned. I knew that they would just think I had schizophrenia because of their limited understanding of the spirit realm. I felt totally helpless. Even my Reiki teacher couldn't help me – he advised me to go to the forest to 'ground' myself, and do more occult practices.

Light Shines Into the Darkness

During this time, God was trying to get my attention. He orchestrated a series of events which led me to realise that I was demon possessed. One of the main things that caused cracks in the deception I was under was 'twin flame' teaching. I couldn't understand why the spirit kept giving me signs that a happily married man was my so-called twin flame. Even a psychic had confirmed it. I also just found out that my cousin, who was involved in Spiritualism, had developed schizophrenia, along with two of my New Age friends. I started to wonder why all of these people doing New Age practices didn't seem stable, even though they were doing so much spiritual work on themselves. Then, I met someone who said he used to practise 'astral projection' with his friends. He said they had bumped into things on the astral plane and had all gone insane. He was the only one who survived. Was I next?

One day, I was walking down the street listening to a Tarot card reader on YouTube, looking for answers. Suddenly I heard the sound of someone screaming in the back of the video. That was the straw that broke the camel's back. It sounded otherworldly, as though someone was being tortured in hell. I had to rewind it a few times just to check what I was hearing. I had been taught that demons were just a part of my inner world, my 'shadow self'. I thought back to a time when I had woken up in the night and seen demons in my room. I suddenly remembered the time when I had played the Ouija board, then I remembered when I had been on paranormal investigations and then the times I took psychedelics and saw DMT 'machine elves' and 'aliens'. I remembered the time I felt something enter my body during meditation, and the many times that ex-partners had told me that I looked demon possessed in the night, doing unusual things. One time, my friend told me that I was asleep, but my legs were straight up in the air, like something was pushing them back. I saw that Christians on YouTube were saying that the Kundalini was a demon.

I suddenly realised demons were real. I had been tricked. The Kundalini *was* a demon, and I was *not* God; I was a sinner. My New Age rose-coloured spectacles fell off and smashed – I saw that evil was not an illusion, like I had been taught. The world was dirty, and so was I. How could I have been so deceived? All of this time, I thought I was serving God and being guided by angels. The facade of the New Age crumbled before my very eyes. I realised that *Jesus was real*, and so was the devil.

I fell to my knees and the fear of the Lord came over me. I cried out to Jesus in desperation, knowing that I needed him to save me, not just from demonic possession but from my sins. I needed forgiveness for the life I had lived in order to be made right with God. I knew Jesus had died for me on the cross. My sins flashed before my eyes and I did my first round of confession. I then found myself listening to a Christian deliverance prayer on YouTube. As the pastor commanded the Kundalini spirit to come out in the name of Jesus, I felt the bottom of my spine start to tingle. Then, what felt like a snake moved slowly down both of my legs and came out of my feet. I was shocked. I lay on my bed crying.

After a few moments, the Holy Spirit came upon me. It felt a bit like a very strong, warm, healing electricity all over my body, like being dipped in warm honey. It was like every cell of my being came alive. It was completely different from the Kundalini electricity. The Kundalini felt more like a dirty drug high, which was overbearing and even felt sexual at times. The Holy Spirit was totally different. He felt pure, clean, loving and holy. I felt like Jesus was standing there with a blowtorch burning all of the demons out of me. I knew I was forgiven and that God was extending his mercy to me. After this, I heard thousands of people screaming in hell. It sounded like a football stadium. I knew God was showing me what he had saved me from.

I confessed my sins and gave my life to Jesus. After that, I was unable to do the things I used to do and had the fear of the Lord. I was unable to listen to the same music, to laugh at the same unclean jokes or watch anything dark. I threw out all of my immodest clothing and started dressing more conservatively. I got rid of my occult books and started reading the Bible. I was delivered from many lifelong strongholds, like lust and sex addiction. Like all Christians, I am a work in progress, but I am a new creation in Christ. God gave me a hunger for the Bible, which suddenly came alive. I started to have encounters with God and experienced the Holy Spirit guiding me and teaching me things. I saw God answer many of my prayers and do many miracles, including healing my friend of motor neurone disease after receiving prayer at the church. I have got so many testimonies of the great things God has done for me, that I could write a whole book about it!

Battles and Baby Steps

I will not pretend that everything was perfect. My ordeal was over, but not quite. All of the Kundalini fire and electricity left after listening to the prayer, which was when the diarrhoea, chronic vomiting and electrocution stopped, but it took some time before

I could make coherent sentences and form thoughts properly. I felt like I'd been in a spiritual car crash and was now in recovery. When I tried to speak, the words and letters were often coming out in the wrong order. I suddenly had a very bad stutter too. My memory was so bad that I felt like I had dementia. It took some time for my stomach to heal too. I also felt like I had binoculars on and my vision was such a mess that I could not even recognise myself in the mirror. I couldn't feel my legs or even tell the difference between the hot and cold tap at times. It seemed like my nervous system and brain had been totally fried, but I was just grateful that I was no longer demon possessed and that being electrocuted every day by the strange fire had stopped. This was a blessing, as I was able to spend time reading the Bible.

After I left the occult, the dark forces turned on me. For many weeks, I had terrible nightmares and sleep paralysis. One night, I woke up and was being strangled by a hand. I got so scared to go to sleep that I decided to pray for protection before bed. Immediately, God answered my prayer and all of the attacks and nightmares stopped from that day on.

I also ended up homeless for a while, but God guided my steps and provided for me all along the way. I was eventually blessed with a beautiful place of my own, and God opened a door for me to study at Bible college. I started to go out on the streets preaching the gospel, praying for the sick and casting out demons on Zoom calls. I also joined a street ministry called Heaven's Kitchen, where a group of Christians go into the city and feed the homeless. God also led me to a group of evangelists and we started travelling the UK, preaching the gospel in different cities. I am excited for what God has in store for me, and for you too. The Christian life is an adventure.

My spirit grieved for those who didn't yet know Jesus as their Lord and Saviour, especially those trapped in the New Age deception and those pursuing spiritual enlightenment, not realising that the so-called highest path is actually the highway to hell. I started exposing the New Age deception on YouTube and making leaflets to reach people.

'Then Peter said unto them, Repent, and be baptised every one of you in the name of Jesus Christ for the remission of sins, and ye shall receive the gift of the Holy Ghost.' (Acts 2:38 KJV)

Candice-Marie's Story

As a child growing up, I would often find myself staring out of the window at the night sky, wondering what time my mother would roll in drunk. The same thought would inhabit my mind as I gazed out at the stars and the heavens. 'There's got to be more than this tiny little moment,' where I felt so lost and alone. There had to be something greater.

I wasn't raised in any faith, in fact I was raised more so by superstitious beliefs, and what I knew about religion stirred no appetite for the soul. After all, what was so gracious and appealing about hearing stories of drunk clergymen cheating on their wives and living seemingly double standards?

Yet, here I was, at the tender age of ten, cowering in the corner of a room, hiding from paramedics in case they took me away. With no one to cling to, no one to ask for help, instinctively praying on my knees to God to not let my mother die from another attempted suicide episode. As I continued to be raised and pruned by trauma, that memory where God did in fact have mercy on my mum became a distant one, though something I would later reflect on.

I lost many years in my teens and twenties to a life of debauchery and hedonism. I've since discovered that this is a common trajectory for untethered and traumatised people who try to fill the God-shaped hole with what the world offers them.

A New Country and a New Family

I met my (now ex) husband whilst studying in London and we ended up getting married and moving to Hong Kong where we began our family. We had our first child in 2013, with no complications. With both of us eager to grow our family, it wasn't long before I became pregnant again, and in June 2015 we welcomed our son into the world. At only one week old he very suddenly died and in an instant, our whole life was turned upside down. The post-mortem gave no cause of death, and just like that the baby I grew inside me for nine months was no more. No praying was going to bring him back. I couldn't even think to pray as it all happened so quickly. I became comfortably numb, a dead person existing in a breathing body, yet there was no trace of life or light. As you can imagine, the loss itself was devastating, and an event that would direct my steps towards the New Age movement.

During this time of intense grief, our firstborn was just nineteen months old. One day, as I watched her bury her head in the sofa, responding to her mother's sudden emptiness and disdain, a sense of panic came over me. I thought to myself that I was going to lose her as the happy child I knew if I didn't pull myself from the inner grave I had sunken into. From that moment forward, I knew my tears had to be put aside.

Searching and Seeking

I began to search for answers, for meaning to this travesty, to try to make sense of such loss and to ease the pain in any way I could. The New Age world had more answers than I ever could have imagined. Little did I know, all these answers were nothing but a mere counterfeit. A counterfeit that would open me up to demonic influences and set me on a path that nearly cost me my life, not just once but multiple times.

It started with seemingly innocent energy medicine, to try to help with the pain I was feeling. I began reading lots of books by New Age spiritual teachers such as Eckhart Tolle, whose teachings emphasised being present with all that you feel.

Before long I had slipped much deeper into New Age spirituality, trying more and more modalities and practices, in an attempt to heal my grief. Here are some of the things I engaged in before I was saved: quantum healing; Reiki, Tarot cards; yoga; Buddhism,

Tantric sexual healing, blood magic, shamanic journeying, plant medicine ceremonies (iboga, peyote, mushrooms, DMT, ayahuasca); sound healing; moon worship; breathwork; astral projection; Transcendental Meditation; Human Design; and chanting. I also became a qualified Kambo practitioner.

Whilst there were moments of elation, the extreme highs were followed by periods of anxiety. Some of the plant medicine ceremonies can be very dangerous. They can re-traumatise a person, not to mention the risk of death, especially when psychedelics are involved.

Furthermore, I discovered that because I had illegally accessed the spirit realm, I had given demons legal rights to torment me. This is why the Word of God tells us not to practise such things. He wants to protect us from seeing such things.

Deepening Pain, Deepening Seeking

My husband and I, still grieving, decided to leave Hong Kong and have a fresh start in Australia. Soon after, we gave birth to our third child and he unexpectedly nearly died twice within the first three weeks of his life. Both events were unconnected and with no apparent cause, further adding trauma to us, and fuelling the need to look for deeper meaning and understanding about life.

Shortly after this, my husband's sister committed suicide, leaving her three teenage boys behind. To help the family, this meant we had to relocate back to England from Australia and I felt so much grief, more than I knew what to do with. The burden of stress from all the traumatic events led to my husband and I separating. I was mentally and emotionally exhausted and now a single mum to a three-year-old and seven-month-old.

I shared my struggles with an old friend, who was a year post divorce, and he suggested I come to one of his 'spiritual circles'. I was reassured that I should 'trust the process'. So in my brokenness, and because I was desperate and willing to try anything to heal the years of grief, in 2018 I walked naively into what would be the most mind-bending and twisted experience of my life. My first plant medicine ceremony involved working with iboga, which is extracted from the Tabernanthe iboga plant, native to Gabon. This was one of the most intense plant ceremonies a person can participate in and I would need a few more chapters to be able to explain what takes place during these ceremonies.

When you take iboga, you are told by the 'shaman' that a lesson will follow the ceremony to test your resolve. After my first ceremony my heart slowed right down, my lips went pale, and it felt like my body was giving up on me. I genuinely thought I was going to die. The team had me stay longer to monitor me while they played down how bad I was. They only told me the next day how severely in danger I had been. I thought I was rising into more light and had passed the test!

The ceremony leaders told me I had the gift of being psychic, and they were 'right'. I believed I was 'channelling' information from the universe, but instead I was receiving information from unclean spirits whose only intention was to deceive me and lead me away from God.

I became a professional in the New Age world. An example of how I would use my 'psychic' abilities is that I would be sitting in a park, in Hertfordshire, doing 'readings' for people in Los Angeles. I would know what their hair was like, what musical instrument they played and what their issues were. These were people I had never met or spoken to, and all they would give me was their first name.

After doing readings, I was invited to attend a private, team-only ceremony, as a practice run for me to become one of them – more like, join their cult! During a hands-on healing session, I collapsed, and everyone believed I was dead. I have no memory of what happened but I was told that I banged my head. I only remember coming back into my body and seeing blackness before my vision and then my hearing returned, with sounds of them calling my name. They believed I had been 'gone' for about fifteen minutes and the next day, when I was fully coherent, no one would look me in the eye as they were all deeply shocked by the experience. I am grateful this meant I never did join their team. In fact, these so-called friends distanced themselves from me and never wanted to talk to me about what happened.

This incident left no trauma in me because of the way it happened. When I look back, I can see that all along God stopped me being fully entrenched in that world, no matter how hard I tried. This is just one of many examples of how I 'almost' became a full-time medicine woman.

I had some very strange experiences during these years in the New Age. One time I was lying in my bed and a dark presence that I can only describe as a black cloud of smoke came over me and pressed down on my chest. I felt like I couldn't breathe. In the New Age you are taught to believe these experiences are normal and an opportunity to stand in your sovereign power, witnessing the release of density as you embody more light. These clouds of black smoke and oppressive experiences are commonly known as 'dark entities' by New Agers.

Message of Doom

Fast forward a few years to May 2021 and I had received a Tarot card reading. The Tower of Babel card was pulled, which symbolises sudden change and crisis. I was told by the card reader that the rug would be pulled out from beneath my feet and that I would lose all my foundations.

That same month the rental property I lived in was put up for sale and I was unable to secure a rental within the area of my children's school. My ex-husband had legally stopped me from moving to another district so I had no other choice except to move back to my hometown in Wales.

This relocation coincided with active family court hearings with my ex-husband, and the children were temporarily ordered to live with him before I returned to Wales. My lawyer said that in her twenty-year career she had never seen anything like this happen before. The hearing wasn't even a final hearing, so no change of residency should have taken place, especially as their father did not live a commutable distance to keep the children in their school.

One phone call and my whole life was changed by people who I had never even met. Within the space of forty-eight hours, I had to say goodbye to my children and what had been our home for the last two and a half years.

Opening to God

Shortly before leaving, I remember that I was lying in bed and something in me guided me to stop praying to different god figures, angels or healing frequencies, but instead pray only to the Holy Spirit. A sense of peace enveloped me and, in a flash, I saw how there *was* a God and he was my spiritual Father who had been there protecting me all along. These experiences are hard to put into words but the sense of peace I felt was like no other. It was like my spirit and soul finally felt they had arrived home.

I had always carried a seed of suspicion in my mind whilst engaging in New Age practices, due to the nature and intensity of them. I wondered where it all ended, and if I would ever get to the point of living in peace and acceptance. At the time I held my 'ego' accountable for these concerns, as another goal in the New Age is to destroy the ego. These processes of 'self-healing' and 'ego-deaths' came with a price tag of anxiety and panic. I was always feeling an urge to do 'the next thing' to improve myself, not to mention the physical price tag to pay for all these 'services'.

Since I was now back in Wales and far removed from this group of gurus and 'spiritual' friends, I had less exposure to the New Age and, as my doubt was only ever increasing by this point, I decided to have a little break from most of my spiritual practices. It is very common for people who are trying to move away from the New Age and towards God, to find themselves experiencing some sort of backlash from the enemy. The enemy will do anything to keep you from having a personal relationship with God, even trying to bring people to a premature death.

The Crash

In September 2021, I was in a freak car accident. There were no other vehicles involved, and my car ended up

flipping three times, landing upside down. I remember
spinning in the air in slow motion and saying to
myself, 'You are fully in a car accident now and there
is no turning back.' As I found myself hanging upside
down, still strapped in by my seat belt, I could smell
burning and thought, 'Right, you're alive, you have
kids, you need to get out of the car!' I unbuckled
myself and climbed through the smashed window on
the driver's side. The crazy thing is that every airbag
went off, apart from mine.

By some miracle everything I needed, like my bag and
phone, was already across the road. I tried to ring 999
for an ambulance but it didn't work, so I just sat on
the side of the road laughing hysterically, in shock,
staring at the upside-down car thinking, 'How on
earth am I alive?!' Eventually a young couple came by
who called the emergency services. Whilst I had a lot
of blood splattered over me, I only had a minor cut on
my ankle due to the broken glass cutting me whilst
getting out of the car, and a few nicks on my hand. So
apart from needing to get my ring cut off my finger,
which was swollen from the impact, I was discharged
from hospital with no concerns.

Whilst I looked physically fine, my health went into
serious decline after the accident and I ended up
pretty much bedbound, at times needing to crawl to
the toilet as the fatigue was so severe. I went from
being a very physically fit and active person, to barely
being able to walk. When I did go for short walks,
it would leave me needing another few days in bed

to regain my energy. I would be in the most horrific pain in my body, which I can only describe as my bones and brain feeling like they were on fire. The time in bed gave me an opportunity to reflect, and my curiosity about my life in the New Age grew. Where were my New Age friends now who were all 'love and light'? Where was the healing now that I couldn't engage in these practices or even meditate because the exhaustion was so extreme? I could barely even open my eyes.

Crossing the Bridge

I came across The Bridge Facebook group in September 2021, which is for people who are, or were, in the New Age but who have questions about it and Jesus. I was thankful to see I wasn't the only one questioning what on earth I had been involved with. It was here that I got a recommendation for a church in my local area.

I went to the church for the first time that same month and shyly hid at the back. All I can say is that once the worship began, I spent the whole time crying my eyes out. It felt like tears of relief. I could tell I was in the right place and that I was meant to be there, whilst also thinking, 'Who are all these insanely happy people singing their hearts out to Jesus?' I gave my life to Jesus that day through saying the sinner's prayer. I didn't know what was going to happen, just that I needed to do it.

Whilst my health still wasn't great and I was spending a lot of time in bed, I began to immerse myself in 'New Age to Jesus' testimonies. Whenever the person spoke about Jesus, it was palpable how moved they were by knowing him. I would find myself crying with them, sharing in the love and peace they felt through Jesus. Overnight, people would relinquish all their practices and make drastic life-changing choices. For some people with large New Age businesses, this meant losing hundreds of thousands of pounds, yet they did it in a heartbeat to follow Jesus. I couldn't get my head around it, but my heart was open, and I became driven to know him and why he had such a profound impact on people's lives.

The Holy Spirit began to work in me, revealing things about myself, and I found myself on my knees in deep repentance, confessing my sins. This time was different from when I had said the sinner's prayer. I felt convicted in my spirit and heart. Tears began to pour out of my eyes as all my sinful ways began to flash before me. It was tough to see and realise the deception I had been a part of but I was so thankful to have been forgiven.

That day I got rid of all New Age books and objects from the house, and in June 2022, whilst away in Tenby, I came across a Christian bookshop and this is when I bought my first ever Bible. Although I was completely unfamiliar with scripture, I woke up one morning with the words 'John 14:6' in my mind, which prompted me to open my Bible to that verse. There, boldly, were the words: 'I am the way and the truth and the life. No one comes to the Father except through me.' When I read this, it was like truth being etched into every fibre of my being and soul.

Whilst I knew the existence of God and my perception was changing, it didn't happen instantaneously for me, as I had seen for others. I still had so many questions. A series of events unfolded which offered confirmation after confirmation about his existence and his love for me. My lingering doubts and confusion began to dissolve. These experiences just kept drawing me closer to him, until eventually the scales were completely removed from my eyes.

God speaks in many ways, and one day he sent a man to reaffirm that God was with me. I was sitting in a coffee shop and this man came over and said, 'God told me to tell you to keep going, that he has his hand over your life and all you need to do is keep seeking him.' I was gobsmacked!

Then one day I was on the M4 driving back home with my children, when all of sudden the cars ahead were slamming on their brakes. I braked hard, but I could tell I wasn't going to stop in time, and I had to make a split-second decision to move into the middle lane without being able to check if it was safe to do so. My daughter began to cry as we swerved lanes but we were safe. As we carried on driving, a few hundred yards down the motorway I saw a sign to my left that said, 'Jesus saves lives'. Again, I was gobsmacked! It was hard to believe – when do you ever see a sign like this on a motorway? But there it was. I began to laugh and weep, knowing once again Jesus had saved my life and my children's also this time.

Confirmation

In September 2022, a friend's brother and wife lost their baby in utero. I had already sensed this would happen as I'd had a dream where I saw myself screaming and having a panic attack in my garden where I received this tragic and specific news. Well, that is exactly what happened: I got the news and was hyperventilating in my garden shortly after.
We decided to go for a walk that day to help digest the news. We pulled up to a very small empty car park and I spent some time sitting on the bench, looking out at the sea, contemplating life. I had more questions for God in the aftermath of such difficult news, wondering why such things happen. Once we finished our walk we headed back to the car park, and there right in front of my very eyes appeared a sign saying 'Jesus Loves You', and next to the hand-painted sign rested a book. The front cover depicted Jesus holding the face of a child, surrounded by three other children and it was titled, *What a Friend We Have in Jesus*. I couldn't believe my eyes and I wept feeling so comforted by his presence.

The love and reassurance Jesus kept offering me broke down all my armour and he began to clean up the internal chaos I had known my entire life. One day, during a church service, God spoke a word to me that he was never going to let me go and that I was his daughter.

The fullness of Jesus encompassed every space in my heart, and in that redefining moment, I absolutely knew the truth of Jesus Christ, and my life has never been the same again since.

It has only been three years of coming to know Christ and already he has changed me in ways that I never thought possible. He took my wounds from the root and softened and healed my heart, changing my view of the world and people. As well as saving my physical life many times, as I have shared in this testimony, and saving my soul from the New Age, God has healed and delivered me from post-concussion syndrome, fibromyalgia, temporomandibular joint dysfunction, complex post-traumatic stress disorder, nightmares, sleep paralysis, rage, panic attacks, self-abandonment, narcissistic traits, seeking validation from others and much more. The closer I position myself to him, the more he refines my character. I've walk in humility since knowing him. I'm now much more aware of my own weaknesses as well as those of others, which has increased my compassion towards humanity and deepened my understanding about why we all need a Saviour.

Having a personal relationship with the One who created me has set me free, no longer succumbing to my flesh and living dead in sin, but living righteously in joy, peace and love, with eternal life. I now know my identity isn't anchored in interchangeable relationships or the riches of the world, but rather in the love that God has for me, his daughter.

My prayer, for those reading this, is for you to accept the gift of salvation and to know that you are so precious to God that you were purchased with the blood of the Son of God, and he is just waiting with all-forgiving and loving arms for you to return home.

Charlotte's Story

As the eldest of four children, growing up I felt the pressure to be the sensible one, my mother's right-hand woman looking after the younger ones. I was also rewarded with maternal praise for stepping into this role. My mother was a traditional woman, clever, competent with low tolerance for incompetence or 'navel-gazing', and a general air of 'everyone should just get on with it'.

My father was an entrepreneur, who suffered from depression and a crippling sense of low self-worth which he medicated with alcohol. Although I was born in Kent in the UK, when I was six months old, my parents emigrated with me to Africa. My sister was born there and my father's building business did well. We lived a materially comfortable life. I have only vague memories of sunshine, a tree-house and a swimming pool at my nursery school.

Back to the UK

Just under five years later, my family fled back to the UK when trouble escalated as a result of the civil war. I was about five years old and I remember being distraught that I left my big, cuddly bunny on the aeroplane. My mum was pregnant with my brother and we lived for a short while with my grandparents in London and then moved to the south coast of England. My dad lost all his money and his business. We had to start from scratch.

My youngest sister completed the family and, although finances were tight, we lived a pretty much average, middle-class life in a small town in England. At my school, we sang hymns at assembly in the mornings and put the nativity on every year. I remember how I loved the nativity story as a child. My mum took us to church at Christmas and Easter but otherwise we didn't discuss religion or spirituality.

There was often disruption at home. Dad was scary, angry and sometimes violent when drunk. He and mum argued. My siblings and I often argued and fought. Conversely, there was also a lot of laughter, fun and raucousness. It was a loud, busy, emotionally volatile household.

My childhood coping mechanism was to hide my emotions and pretend I was unaffected even when I was deeply upset. When things were out of control and scary at home, I felt I had to be strong for my younger siblings.

My mum made us say the Lord's Prayer every night before bed. I think perhaps because her parents did this with her. She was more on the atheist side of agnostic. She valued intelligence and academic achievement and I wanted to prove myself to her, so worked hard enough to do well at school.

A reliable woman, my mum was physically available for me and my siblings. She would pick us up from school and drive us everywhere we needed to go. She clothed, dressed and fed us well. However, emotionally, she had little sympathy for us, unless it was something she deemed serious like physically injuring ourselves. (I once, in desperation, told her that some friends were bullying me and she waved me away like an annoyance.)

Dad was not reliable. He was troubled. He often would forget to pick me up from school, leaving me the last, lonely child miserably waiting at the school gates. At that age, around seven years old, I had no concept of adult problems and to my young mind, the evidence all pointed to just one conclusion – he didn't love me.

At primary school, we were told the story of Zacchaeus, the tax collector, and how Jesus chose to go to *his* house. For some reason, this story stayed with me and I was taken, even at that young age, with how Jesus chose a 'bad man' and the impact he had on a 'bad man'. I had a childlike belief in God – I just took it for granted that he existed.

Childlike Faith Turns to Atheism

When I was twelve, I was profoundly affected watching a science programme on TV. (I think it was talking about astronomy and perhaps the Big Bang.) My world turned topsy-turvy as I experienced a paradigm shift and what felt like a realisation that God doesn't exist. A horrible thought landed: 'Everything is only here by accident.' This burrowed its way into my brain and remained firmly embedded. For the next eighteen years, I embraced atheism.

During that time, I would argue with Christians. I thought they were boring, 'goody-goody' and seeking the comfort of a lie. Christianity, as far as I was concerned, was backward, and religion was used to control people. In my prideful nature I thought I was too clever to be a Christian.

Passing my O levels, I went on to sixth-form college to do A levels and I took Sociology. The work of Karl Marx and the feminist movement had a great influence on me. This bedded in my firm hatred of religion and the patriarchy. I then went on to university. I drank and partied my way through those three years, with a nod to some studying in between. I achieved my degree but didn't especially apply myself. It felt like a badge I needed to get. I wasn't overly interested in it.

What I was interested in was boys. I had a fantasy of falling in love with Mr Right and living happily ever after. Unfortunately, I was more in love with the 'idea of Mr Right' than actually meeting someone, getting to know them and actually demonstrating love. I thought that falling in love and being loved by my perfect man would solve all my problems. That became the answer.

And I did fall in love several times. I was emotionally immature, struggling with alcohol, and my relationships would inevitably go wrong. I craved the high of the honeymoon period. I loved that – when it felt like I was on top of the world no matter what was going on in the rest of my life. I wanted to feel like that all the time. Unrealistically, I somehow believed that if it was 'real love' it would feel like that all the time.

So I kept seeking that 'love high' and leaving relationships when things got too messy. With a fear of abandonment and a dread of rejection, I'd leave before they left me. I gravitated to men who cheated on me and treated me poorly.

Drinking, taking recreational drugs and clubbing, I was always the last one standing at a party. Yet, it was a bleak time. I experimented with morality. Being a deep thinker, internally I was exploring ideas of right and wrong. There was a period where I figured it just didn't matter what I or anyone else did. There was no standard. No objective moral standard. Convincing myself that it was 'just for fun', I had an affair with a married man. (Not fun – actually very painful and desperately sad.)

At last, feeling beaten down and hurt after a string of damaging relationships, I concluded that, even in a world without God, morals and values were important. I tried to do better but didn't have the understanding that I was warring against a sin nature.

I kept trying to be perfect and yet I lived a double life, maintaining this model 'front' during working hours and yet drinking and doing drugs behind closed doors.

Seeking the Supernatural

After a painful bereavement, I really started to question my view that there was no afterlife. A few things happened at once. I don't remember exactly which order but the bereavement was pivotal. I became obsessed with spirit-medium programmes on TV – at the time, Jon Edwards and Colin Fry were big and I hungrily watched every episode. Although an atheist, I had still been open to the supernatural – I'd wondered about platform mediumship and figured it was some kind of telepathy, perhaps using parts of our brain that we don't normally use.

Now, I watched and I wondered – could they actually be talking to our dead loved ones? Then I had a phone call from a friend who didn't know I had experienced a loss – but she had been to see a spirit-medium who had a message for me. She left me a message to say that my loved one was safe and well. My friend told me things in that message that there was no way she could have known. I fell to my knees and broke down in tears. But relief flooded me because from that point on I had hoped that my lost loved one was okay and that there was somewhere else that we went when we died. Somewhere good.

My brother was into Eastern mysticism and spirituality and I went to a bookshop to buy him a birthday present. I thought it was all pretty much nonsense. But while I was browsing in the spiritual section of the store, I saw a book on the shelf called *Conversations with God*. I shuddered at the word 'God'. I felt very uncomfortable with anything that resembled a religious God. But I felt an 'intuitive nudge' to pick up the book. I told myself that I would open it at a random page and if I liked what I read I would buy it. I opened it at a random page and it said something like, 'If you're looking for God in a particular place, you might just miss *her*.' As an angry and slightly militant feminist at the time, I liked that and so I bought the book.

As I started to read it, I devoured every page, and by the end I was convinced that God was real and I became 'spiritual but not religious'. This was not the God of the Bible, but I didn't know that at the time. I assumed that it was the same God and my hatred towards Christianity evaporated. However, I was still fundamentally against organised religion. Yearning for meaning and purpose in my life, I became a spiritual seeker, attending courses, talks and workshops to learn about 'spirituality'.

Getting in Deeper

Working in the corporate world, I'd become disenchanted with a career in financial services. I turned my thoughts to carving out a living providing holistic health services. While still working full time, I trained in Reiki, then reflexology and finally embarked on a four-year course studying homeopathy.

Becoming very health conscious, I was careful to eat nutritious food, I researched pharmaceutical drugs and avoided taking any medication unless absolutely necessary. Ironically, I was still drinking alcoholically and occasionally taking recreational drugs. My long-term relationship broke down and after separating from my partner, my drinking escalated.

Realising I was very broken, I was now on a 'healing mission'. Singing bowl healing, crystals, quantum hypnosis, homeopathy, Reiki, past-life regressions, spirit mediums and angel card readings – you name it, I did it. Being into New Age and New Thought philosophies, I also fully subscribed to the belief that I could heal myself. And that I had all the answers within.

During a therapy session, my counsellor recommended I try a twelve-step recovery programme. On 1st

January 2011, I had my last alcoholic drink. The fact that it was 1.1.11 meant a lot to me because I was interested in 'angel numbers'!

Recovery programmes have their faults, but there were two hugely important factors which had a significant impact on me. First, I surrendered to God and I learnt to pray to God for help. (I witnessed answers to some of these prayers.) Second, all the denial and sense that I was a 'good person' shattered, it became abundantly clear how dreadful my thinking and behaviour had been all my life. (In biblical terms I became aware of my sin nature.) Even though I had surrendered and prayed to God, I was still very much rooted in New Age beliefs at this time and didn't have any real understanding of who God is.

Moving on with my life, sober, my conduct improved immensely and I started living by a moral compass. Life became more manageable.

Spiritual advancement became important to me. I did 'shadow work' – admitting, uncovering and working to change the darker elements of myself. I studied mindfulness and meditation, becoming a meditation teacher. As much as I hated religion, I enrolled on a multi-faith training course (after receiving 'signs' from the universe).

I read 'spiritual books' voraciously – *The Power of Now* and *The New Earth* by Eckhart Tolle, *The Celestine Prophecy,* a whole range of New Age and New

Thought authors including Wayne Dyer, David Wilcox, Fritjof Capra and Neale Donald Walsh.

Channellers and channelled information became my 'go to' source of wisdom. Material channelled from the Pleiadeans and the Arcturians – supposedly 'advanced alien races' with messages for humanity.

A friend loaned me her library of Dolores Cannon books – transcripts of conversations with people who under hypnosis claimed they were 'aliens' in previous lives.

Throughout these numerous works, across each different author, four core messages were consistently repeated. Promises of:

1. a new earth coming,
2. a human ascension (for those who were ready to ascend) to a new earth in the fifth dimension,
3. a great shift soon happening,
4. a day when the spiritual dimension would freely interact with the physical dimension.

The New Age Becomes My Identity

A spiritual teacher of mine recommended Abraham Hicks (a 'collective consciousness' – supposedly of advanced spiritual beings – channelled by a woman called Esther Hicks). I watched their videos avidly and learned about the 'Law of Attraction'. According to this teaching, anything that happened in my life, I had 'attracted'. So if it was bad or difficult or challenging, it was because I wasn't thinking positive thoughts or visualising my perfect life clearly enough.

Manifestation and visualisation workshops littered my diary. And my manifestation practices started working. I would visualise a particular job or house and it would appear in my life. Getting these results was the confirmation I needed that this was all true. Slowly, the idea of a personal God was eroded from my mind. God was 'source', impersonal, disinterested, nebulous – a force, an energy not a person. I now looked down my nose at the simple prayer life recommended in recovery, calling it 'kindergarten spirituality'. I was far more spiritual than that, I decided.

Working as a meditation teacher, I started engaging in meditation and visualisation practices 'to meet my spirit guides'. I would write questions about my life on a piece of paper and then meditate, emptying my mind before 'free-form' writing to get the answers. Reading back what I'd written, I was astonished by the wise messages, the advice that worked and puzzled also by sometimes strange instructions (for example, 'You must do what we tell you, even if it seems odd, signed the Lords of Karma').

With all the energy healing, meditation and manifesting I was doing, I was having more and more supernatural experiences. Convinced this meant I was progressing, I doubled-down even harder. My aim was to raise my vibration, to ascend and become enlightened. My goals were to become wise beyond measure, to gain supernatural powers and, most importantly, attain continuous inner peace.

Ah, that illusive inner peace. I chased it. At workshops, during various practices or while I was having certain spiritual 'treatments', I would experience feelings of ecstasy, bliss and euphoria. I would sometimes feel such love and joy for everyone and everything. In those moments, I felt 'this was it' or I was nearly there. Without fail, these feeling states would eventually fade, lasting anything from one hour to three weeks. (Looking back now, I see that I may have been sober, but I'd found a new drug!)

My research led me to the 'Ascended Masters' – apparently humans who had once walked the earth, had now ascended and achieved enlightenment so they no longer needed to reincarnate on earth. These included Buddha, Confucius and Jesus. I learned they still worked with us from the spiritual realm and were trying to assist other humans to ascend. And I discovered that this enlightened state, called 'Christ Consciousness', was the real 'Second Coming' and a state we could all attain if we worked for it.

Opening to 'Trutherism'

With a new passion for healthy living, my research led me to the corruption in the multi-billion-pound pharmaceutical industry with their conflicting drivers of improving people's health versus profit. I read about unethical experimentation that had been sanctioned by the American government. In 2007, my sister's boyfriend loaned me a video called *Zeitgeist* (a 9/11 conspiracy film) and then a David Icke book. Angry and indignant at the way 'they' (the elites) were conspiring against 'us', I became a fervent (and somewhat annoying) Truther.

By around 2014, this obsession had dissipated. My dad died, I left the corporate world and started working in a self-employed role in the funeral industry, which felt meaningful and worthwhile. I met a decent man and we settled into a nice house of our own. I had some good friends and continued with my meditation and spiritual interests in my spare time. Life was happy.

My interest in Hermeticism, Gnosticism and the 'mystery schools' was ignited. These philosophies promised secret knowledge that if only I could learn, and practices which if only I could become adept at, would result in my ascension.

On YouTube, I listened to a spiritual teacher who had studied ancient texts including the Bible. Much as I thought it was the most boring book on the planet (never having read it!) and I felt a sense of revulsion when I tried to read it, I was open to the idea that it too contained 'hidden spiritual knowledge' to be uncovered if read in the right way. I started following a speaker online and then booked in some mentoring sessions with him. I knew he was a Christian but I didn't know what that actually meant. (I thought *I was* a Christian, a Buddhist and a Jew . . .)

During one session I told my mentor about a strange and frightening supernatural experience I'd had when I'd seen a skeletal entity, floating in mid-air. 'If you ever encounter anything like that,' my mentor told me, 'say to it, "I cast you out in the name of the Lord Jesus Christ." They're terrified of Jesus,' he said.

In March 2020, the UK government announced the lockdown in response to what the world was calling the Covid pandemic. This catapulted me back into the Truther scene. I knew something was very wrong. I found a group of new like-minded friends and we delved into every rabbit hole going, uncovering some real conspiracies and some far-fetched ones. What was clear, was at the bottom of all these conspiracies were Satanists and Luciferians in positions of power dotted throughout society.

The Truther scene is very 'New Age/syncretic' in terms of the spiritual paradigm that is promoted. Echoing in my ears was the constant mantra that 'they' (the perpetrators of all this) were 'afraid' that 'we' (the spiritual Truthers) would 'remember who we really are' and realise 'how powerful we actually are'. When this happened 'their' days would be numbered because 'we' would 'raise our vibration' (reach a certain spiritual/feeling state) and being 'co-creators' of our reality would essentially wipe these 'low vibration' bad guys from existence. It was a seductive thought and gave me hope that the darkness of the world could be eradicated forever, if I did my bit.

The promise was that when a critical tipping point of people had reached a spiritual awakening, evolved to a certain level of consciousness, achieved 'Christ Consciousness' or a certain level of enlightenment (essentially all different ways of saying the same thing), this collective level of consciousness and high vibratory thoughts would actually create a new '5th Dimension' earth.

Not everyone would make it, we were told, but those who were not yet evolved enough would simply reincarnate on a different, lower vibratory planet until they were ready to progress. However, it was our task, 'the lightworkers', the 'starseeds', those 'on the spiritual path' to wake others up and be there for them when they 'woke up' — to help them heal and to guide them. Although I considered myself a kind, compassionate healer who wanted to help others, looking back I can also see how this fed into a sense of being 'spiritually better' or 'more advanced' than others, stroking one's pride again. In other words, 'New Age narcissism'.

Coming out of the 'pandemic period', life seemed to stabilise and I was feeling happy again. It was mid-2021 and I really felt like I knew my purpose and direction in life. My work, my relationships, my spirituality all seemed fulfilling.

There was just one problem.

At night I'd begun experiencing horrifying nightmares, waking several nights a week screaming in terror. This alternated with sporadic episodes of sleep paralysis where I was frozen but awake. Usually, I would wrestle for several minutes against the paralysis until, through the sheer force of my will, I could turn my head, which in turn would release my body. In the mornings, I was finding rows of horizontal scratches all up my forearms. I remember showing my partner and wondering how I'd got them. Could it have been our cat, I wondered? Weirdly, they never seemed to heal properly. Some mornings, I would emerge from a sleep so deep that it was like I'd been unconscious, and yet I felt exhausted. I'd drag myself out of bed and wonder how I was going to get through the day. One morning, as I steadied myself against the wall, almost too tired to hold myself up, I flinched. My body felt tender all over and there was a strange bruised sensation just under my skin.

Feeling increasingly puzzled, I reported these symptoms to my homeopath and asked if she thought I was going through the menopause. She gave me remedies which didn't work.

Breakthroughs and Realisations

As part of my spiritual growth, I embarked on a Tarot card course. My friend and I went for coffee with the

Tarot teacher who told us that her Christian friends were praying for her. I rolled my eyes and huffed: 'I bet it doesn't even say you can't do Tarot in the Bible! In fact, I'm sure Jesus was an astrologer. My mentor knows the Bible, I'll ask him!'

When questioned, my mentor pointed me to Deuteronomy 18:10-12 and explained there was a reason that God forbade these things. 'Demons love that stuff,' he said. Horrified, I put my Tarot cards away in a drawer and abandoned the course.

Meanwhile, I'd started my own spiritual training school, preparing each teaching module drove me to investigate the roots of my own core spiritual beliefs. During the course of my research, I felt a rising panic while studying 'mothers of the New Age' Helena Blavatsky and Alice Bailey, both proponents of 'Christ Consciousness'. Excerpts from their own books revealed they were Luciferians.

Confusion set in. It was becoming increasingly obvious that many of my spiritual beliefs were Luciferian doctrine. 'But surely it can't all be false and evil?' I pondered.

In February 2022, I woke up feeling panicked and in sleep paralysis. I couldn't move or even open my eyes. Suddenly I remembered what my mentor had said, and although I couldn't speak, I thought the words, 'I cast you out in the name of Jesus Christ.' The paralysis stopped instantly. No wrestling, no strain. Just instant.

When I got up the next morning, two BIG questions circled around and around my head. Did this mean the biblical Jesus was true? Was everything I'd learned and believed about spirituality a lie?

In desperation, I said a sincere prayer to God. It went something like this: 'Dear God, I'm so sick and tired of being deceived. Please show me the truth.'

The Veil is Lifted

The following night I had a lucid dream, in which a handsome young man was walking by my side. 'I'm your friend,' he said. 'We've been working together a long time.' I smiled at him and then suddenly feeling suspicious, I said, 'Reveal yourself in the name of Jesus.' At that, he turned into a green-skinned zombie with red eyes. Fear gripped me but I shouted, 'I cast you out in the name of Jesus.' Repeating it a second time, my voice sounded demonic and he disappeared. On the third repetition, I started coughing, and as he came up out of my mouth like smoke, I woke up.

The next morning I felt a sense of freedom. I wasn't sure what had just happened, but I knew I had to throw my Tarot cards away and I ordered a copy of the Bible.

Little did I know what awaited me as I laid my head on the pillow the next night. The cause of my scratches, exhaustion and bruised sensation was finally revealed.

I woke in the middle of the night as a circular-saw-toothed demon latched onto my face and tried to suck the life-force out of me. Again, mentally calling on Jesus caused it to flee.

A couple of days later I was walking down the street in a daze. My whole worldview had come crashing down. My mind struggled to process each of the following thoughts in turn:

- Demons are real.
- So I think Satan must be real.
- In which case God must be REAL.
- And Jesus is REAL!

A thrill shot through me at that last thought and, in the next moment, I got what I can only describe as 'a glimpse of God'. A tiny, split-second glance at his awesome power. All the demons' supernatural powers appeared like parlour tricks in comparison.

With an unfamiliar sense of clarity and certainty, I knew that 'Jesus has authority over demons'. And I knew that God loved me and I knew I didn't deserve it. Many of my flaws surfaced in my mind and I felt truly regretful. I felt I'd let God down. I also understood that God respects free will absolutely, and had allowed me the freedom to dabble with all the many selfish and stupid things I'd done, thinking it would make me happy. I realised that God had never abandoned me and had been with me throughout my life, even as I rejected him. The sense of being loved was overwhelming and a deep peace settled in my heart.

My Bible arrived and I felt an urgency and longing to read it. I started with the book of Matthew and was transported into the account of Jesus's life and ministry; it was like I was there. I cried when Jesus was tortured and crucified. It was all so real. And I knew deep within my soul it was true.

New Life

At this point I didn't know any Christians but God is so good. He quickly brought me into a strong Christian fellowship and settled me into a good church. I was baptised in the sea on the south coast of England in September 2022.

The irony is that the elusive peace I'd worked so hard for twenty years to grasp, has been a free gift from Jesus. No matter how difficult life gets, it's there in the background. Every day I now have the reassuring comfort provided by a relationship with the living God, and the hope of eternity with Jesus on the real 'New Earth' as described in chapter 21 of the book of Revelation in the Bible, where there will be no more sorrow or tears.

If you are reading this and are sceptical or not sure, why not try a very simple prayer: 'Dear God, I don't know what to believe, please show me the truth.'

Jonathan's Story

I had some sort of faith as a young child. I had a Bible (loved Genesis!) and sometimes prayed, so it's beautiful to realise in hindsight that I had a relationship with God. The Narnia books by C.S. Lewis really stick out from when I was growing up. They were the most engrossing things of my childhood. I was transported into this magical land. My grandma was a strong practising Christian, and, for reasons I'll get into later, she was the only adult I experienced unconditional emotional love from. She was a massive part of my childhood, so much so that I used to cry and scream when I had to leave her house after staying there with her for weekends, then having to go back to my own. My home felt like a dark and lonely place without my grandma's love. I wish I could speak to her now I'm a Christian. I feel pretty sad that as I hit puberty, I started making fun of her faith. I started going into full-on rebellion.

Childhood Pain

Rebellion has been a theme of my life, as I'll expand on, but rewinding – at age three and a half, I had meningitis and was in a coma for ten plus days. The doctors told my parents I wasn't likely to wake up or live and to prepare for my passing. I apparently had so much prayer over me while in that coma. I actually remember waking up from it after ten days and feeling fine. I was told much later that I pushed Mum away and wouldn't let her hug me. The only one I let hold me initially, post coma, was my eldest sister, Vanessa. She had been like a surrogate mother to me emotionally as my own mother wasn't able to. Everyone said it was a miracle I survived. It was an impossibility, according to the doctors. I firmly believe God saved me. For the first time.

Some family background – my twelve-year-old brother, Martin, was run over outside of the house I was brought up in, eighteen months before I was born. This defined family life in an unspoken way. Mum had retreated into guilt, grief and anxiety. Martin was the second child she'd lost. She's lost three out of five now.

My parents never spoke to each other once about Martin's death throughout their entire marriage (Mum told me this recently). There was always an underlying darkness and sadness I could sense that I couldn't quite put my finger on. Life definitely felt 'off' from a very early age, right up until encountering

Jesus. There was a black void in my childhood home that I carried in my heart through to adulthood. I do not remember any emotional love or validation, I was never told 'well done' or 'I love you'. In fact, I was always very surprised when I witnessed this in other families. I used to wonder if there was something wrong with me.

I remember the first time Mum negatively compared me to Martin when I was aged five or six, in front of a classmate we were dropping home. Shame engulfed me, I wanted to disappear, and also, I felt hot anger. It was like being stabbed in the heart. This happened throughout my childhood until I smashed the house up aged twelve as a result. It didn't happen again, but I had lost something. It seemed that I was no good and that everything was my fault. My childish soul inhabited a very lonely and sad place. And I thought, 'Well, if I can't be good, what's the point? I may as well be the opposite, at least that way I'm noticed.'

Substances Enter My Life

I really looked up to my eldest sister, Vanessa. I idolised her. She was eleven years older and she seemed so cool as a 'hippy' in CND. Rebelling against the stifling middle-class suburban culture of brushing everything under the carpet and twitching net curtains. She also defended me against Mum negatively comparing me to Martin. When I was six, she became dependent on injecting heroin, a 'junkie', not that I understood what that meant. She became a walking ghost around the family home before leaving at age seventeen. One day she was there and my best friend, the next she was gone.

I remember, as if it were yesterday, intentionally getting drunk for the first time aged six. This was the start of substances becoming a big part of my life, just like my sister's. I often went to visit her in her new 'hippy house' and was given alcohol. I drank whisky at one of her parties and was found passed out in the bath with the bottle at a very young age. I was given my first spliff aged eleven by my middle sister, Kate. Drugs became romanticised in my mind and an obsessional pull for me. I dreamed about doing them long before I actually even took any. If I found a stray tablet in the house, I wondered, fascinated, 'Is this heroin?'

I found a couple of Christian testimony books in the house, attracted to the front cover picture of a flick-knife: *Run Baby Run* by Nicky Cruz and *The Cross and the Switchblade* by David Wilkerson. I must have been around eleven or twelve years old and I devoured the gang part of the testimony. I completely shied away from the conversion parts, not understanding it and thinking it was dull. I loved the rebellious escape and romanticised gangs to the point that I set up my own gang at primary school.

By the time I hit puberty, I was in full-blown rebellion in mind and deed. I had no respect for my father, who

I perceived as weak for not standing up to my mother, while I was at war with my mother. I was thrown out of school just before my GCSEs but managed to go to another place to do my A-Levels. Leaving there at aged eighteen, the first sentence of their report to prospective universities was, 'We do not think Jonathan is a suitable candidate for higher education.' I've since got a Master's degree.

As a teenager I felt so lonely, empty and insecure. My inner anxiety levels were insane, but I soon learnt to make up for it with the magic potion called alcohol. A lot of alcohol, and regularly as a kid. I had a quick wit and brain, which got me friends, but alcohol was the glue that held me together and enabled me to 'live'.

Addiction and death have run through my family line. My great-grandad committed suicide through alcohol, my sister Vanessa died almost four years ago with alcohol being a contributing factor, and some other family members have pretty bad issues as well.

From age sixteen I smoked hash daily, and when I went to university, I sold it from day one. That's how I made my friends that first week as a Fresher. We then all seriously got into raving, being part of the rave generation back in the 1990s. They were my Tribe. My family. My Bachelor's dissertation was on 'How rave has replaced religion in today's youth culture'.

Hedonism and blissful escape were the norm. I would NEVER conform to a society I despised! I was also hyper promiscuous, way beyond anyone else I knew. Anything to try and fill the God-shaped hole.

The Psychedelic Scientist

How did New Age 'spiritual' beliefs come into my life? I did quite a few Ouija boards as a child. The last one we did as teenagers I didn't fully believe, so I took my finger off the glass and asked the spirit a question that no one else knew the answer to – the name of my dead brother. Immediately the glass shot to M A R T I N! 'Spiritual' doors were now open.

At age eighteen I threw a magic mushroom party at my parents' house when they were away. I remember looking in the mirror and seeing the devil looking back at me, which obviously freaked me out. Then I lay down on the carpet and I was pulled down into this fiery red, horrible place, which I don't know how to describe other than it being hell.

After a very fun hedonistic twenties, drugs became my defining identity, one of nihilism. Especially during a long-term eleven-year relationship with a woman very similarly broken to myself. I became like this mad scientist, researching chemicals (I should have a PhD in Psychopharmacology with all the obsessive research I've done). I played God, tweaking my brain this way and that. It became my religion. Drugs were my idol, yet underneath I was incredibly depressed. I coped by always being high in one form or another. I also had a full-on growing porn addiction that went hand in hand with the drugs. I didn't do one without the other.

However, I was seemingly outwardly successful in the world. I had a really good corporate job, owned a penthouse in Clapham, London, had a beautiful girlfriend and loads of party friends. Why did I still feel empty? Oh well, who cares, I'll just keep getting high!

New Age Spirituality

Towards the end of that dramatically toxic relationship, I started to realise that I had quite a bad substance problem and sought help. After we split up, I immediately took myself to rehab. My main takeaway from my time there was my introduction to spirituality. Meditation, predominantly of the Eastern form, had a profound effect on me. I was able to tap into the 'universe' incredibly easily. I'd gone from scientific nihilism to believing we're all one and part of the same 'source'. I soon learnt for myself that the universe was full of spirits and I believed what I learnt from supposedly enlightened practitioners, that anything 'spiritual' had to be good.

I was soon introduced to Shamanism. My addiction psychotherapist was also a shamanic healer. Via shamanic practices with her I met my dead brother on top of a mountain in a drumming ceremony, blindfolded. In fact, I met all three of my dead siblings through shamanic practices. This culminated in me going to the Amazon with her group of cool 'spiritual' misfits, for an 'intensive ayahuasca retreat' with indigenous Peruvian shamans leading the ceremonies and giving us the 'ayahuasca magic potion'.

In one ceremony, I was shot out of my body and flew around the universe. After some time exploring, I got bored of the universe, and becoming homesick I crash landed back on the Amazon jungle floor. An indigenous man appeared and came up to me with a blowpipe, pushed it in my ear and blew insects into my brain. I literally felt them eating away at my brain. It was horrific. You could call it a psychedelic trip but it was a real spiritual experience. I had an earache afterwards and do wonder if my ongoing tinnitus could be related.

I've had so many intense 'spiritual' experiences on psychedelics. After Peru, I got into smoking DMT. I learnt how to interact with 'entities' in the universe, and some of them were really dark. I will never forget the looming, menacing, leering, enormous Aztec Joker entity. I've researched since then that he is a common entity encountered in these realms and I now firmly know it to be a demon. Yet some entities were very beautiful, even playful. The more I toyed with different psychedelics and so-called 'plant medicines', promoted by the New Age culture, the more adept I became at navigating these 'spiritual' realms. I felt I was becoming a sort of god. If I were becoming a god, I certainly didn't need God! Oh, the pride from my ascension up the spiritual ladder.

Breakdown to Lockdown

The drugs, the 'spirituality' and corporate burnout, culminated in me having a breakdown in February 2020. This ended in an intentional overdose and waking up in hospital. I knew then that everything had to change. After thirty years of living in London, I made plans to escape to the countryside, make a new life for myself and start again.

Then March 2020 happened and the period I now call 'The Troubles'. My world was turned upside down, not least by family members not leaving their houses and insinuating I was a murderer for not 'following the rules'. I became an active and known figure in the 'Awake', 'Truther' or 'Freedom Movement'. I was part of the resistance to the global narrative and top down imperatives (tyranny). Research and activism became my full-time occupation after purposefully leaving the corporate world.

This started by logically disproving state propaganda with their own statistics, and both medical and scientific evidence (I'm a bit of a geek really). However, the movement I'd got caught up with and had become a leader in, soon started turning into full-on anarchy. I was also now totally surrounded by New Age 'spiritual not religious' people who talked about '5D ascension', 'lightworkers', 'frequencies', aliens that were on our side, secret knowledge, and so on. Given my shamanic dabbling, I related to this group more than everyone else, who we called 'normies'. However, I also felt different from many of them as I worked more on logic and have a Master's in Science. Something felt off, not only with the mainstream narratives but also with this alternative bunch.

My 'escape from London' plans came to fruition in October 2021 and I moved to Stroud (one of the English 'spiritual' capitals). I was under the influence of psychedelics almost daily and started having a love affair with a green nature goddess in the spiritual realm. I didn't yet know Stroud, yet she astral projected me, flying me around the hills here on a beautiful carpet of green foliage. I got to see and know the area without leaving my bed. This reinforced in me that anything 'spiritual' had to be good. I didn't know any other form of spirituality and that's what the prevailing culture I had surrounded myself with told me.

The astral projection was predominantly under the influence of psychedelics, namely Ketamine at this point. I loved being transported by this beautiful green goddess. I loved her. I just wanted to keep going back for more and more of this spiritual 'bliss', love and acceptance.

On My Knees

Three months after moving to Stroud (I'm sure God brought me here for this reason), my fellow 'Truther' friend Lucinda, recommended a Christian

Truther documentary called *Aethereal* by 'The Truth is Stranger Than Fiction' YouTube documentary maker. It's about Biblical cosmology and the battle for heaven and earth. The last line really hit me. The narrator asked one slow, purposeful question – 'Who do you serve?'

Bang! I had my first encounter with God as an adult. I immediately crumpled to my knees on the floorboards in what I now know to be repentance. I cried my eyes out in remorse as I realised that I'd inadvertently been serving the wrong master throughout my adult life. The paradox was that so were the very same group I'd been resisting and protesting against. It was a trap – I'd been duped! Both sides were controlled – the 'mainstream' and the 'counter movement'.

As a result of going down the many dark rabbit holes that the 'Truther' world opened up for me, I learnt how evil the world is. That there are satanic rituals in plain sight on a global scale. That many of the ruling classes seemed to worship and serve Lucifer/Satan in secret societies, and so on. When you know what to look for, the evidence is everywhere hidden in plain sight. I soon started to understand that Satan and evil really do exist, and if Satan exists, that must mean ... and off I went towards Jesus.

There was also an academic, intellectual side to my conversion. I tried to disprove the Bible, not least the resurrection, historically and intellectually, but I found that I couldn't. It was true beyond reasonable doubt. That was all I needed to satisfy myself on the intellectual side, along with the spiritual experiences with God I was having that were unlike anything I'd experienced before.

I was not without counsel during this time. My pastor and other Christians were very supportive in my waking up to the fact that Jesus is *the truth*. As a 'Truther', I had been 'awake'. Now I was truly awake. The scales had fallen from my eyes. Finally, I could see. Everything was different. All fear and anger left me at this point.

From that point on in December 2021, I became very open to Jesus and started praying and reading the Bible. The prayer I was doing was better than any therapy I'd ever had, and I'd had three years of it, as well as a year's training as a psychotherapist in Psychosynthesis.

The Battle

However, I was still dabbling with the 'other side' here and there. Early 2022 was the last time I did psychedelics. That final time the entities were angry with me. I felt their anger was due to my walk towards Jesus. They pulled off their 'masks' and I saw them as the demons that they are. All the electricity was off in my room, including my speaker, yet a serpent came up and out of the speaker and electrocuted me through both of my little fingers. Afterwards, I knew it was real as my arms ached for a week. The electric current shot from the tips of my little fingers to my elbows. I went insane with fear at the attack and instinctively cried out to Jesus. The whole thing then stopped dead immediately. A physical impossibility given how much Ketamine I'd consumed. I threw all my psychedelics away that night.

I saw that this wasn't some sort of spiritual game I was playing; it was very, very, real. I then realised and knew for sure that the realms I'd been exploring were demonic. As was the whole New Age spiritual side of things, as well as the substances I'd been using to open the spiritual doors to those realms.

My path in life prior to meeting Jesus had just got darker and darker, as I'd inadvertently got tangled up with more and more evil. I had been trying to manage negative childhood family experiences and find my own solutions. Those solutions had included putting a line up my nose every time I left the family home, all those years ago, in despair and sadness after a visit. I had deluded myself that I was in control but knew deep down it was dark. I'd been self-medicating depression and a deep sadness. 'Spirituality' and substances completely returned void. I'd been searching for peace and healing but got more and more into addiction and New Age spirituality as a result.

I thought I'd learnt to access anything I wanted in the spiritual realm, but at the same time I had become more and more isolated. I realise now that

I didn't have access to anything good. I'd closed the doors on the good and opened them up to the bad masquerading as 'light'. If only I had known back then that all I had to do was call on the name of Jesus.

It's not been a smooth journey by any means. Up to this point, I still hadn't fully given myself to Christ as my Lord and Saviour. I'd mostly given up recreational drugs, but I had a shopping list of self-prescribed pharmaceutical 'medications' that I was completely dependent on. I started getting more and more convicted to get off all of these pills. It's probably been the hardest thing I've done in my life, and it's still ongoing. I took Diazepam every day for eighteen years and had a horrific six-month withdrawal. I can attest to the fact that it's the hardest drug in the world to get off. Much harder than heroin for example.

What made me so convicted to come off these so-called medications? Well, they are just part of the soup that was my internal dis-ease of existing in this world. In August 2023, I came to the end of myself. After the inquest into my elder sister Vanessa's death (after her being found unexpectedly dead in her bath in suspicious circumstances), my two-year romantic relationship ending, and an accidental overdose (which I'm convinced God saved my life from), I completely unravelled. I considered suicide rationally for the first time. Only the fear of the Lord stopped me because I thought, if all of this biblical stuff is true, I really don't want to risk ending up in a possibly worse place than this one. I was utterly broken, on my knees again. For the first time completely submitting myself to God. Crying out in desperation – 'I'm done with my way, God, it's over to you, I can't carry on. Help!'

The End of Self is the Beginning of God

The very next day I was given a pastor's number who specialises in addiction. I rang him. It rang and rang and finally he picked up and told me he was on a spa holiday with his wife and had purposefully left his phone in the car for a week. He only came back during the thirty seconds when I phoned to get something his wife had left in the car. What were the chances?

Six weeks later I was in my second rehab to try and start getting off the pharmaceuticals I'd used to 'manage my mental health'. I've since found out that the Greek word 'pharmakeia', warned about five times in the New Testament Bible, means 'poison or magic art or sorcery and witchcraft'. I'd been taking those pills for years and years.

Just before I went into rehab, I went on a joyful prayer walk in the hills behind my house full of hope in God. An incredible rainbow appeared above my head which blew my mind. I now know that signifies God's promises. By the second week in rehab, detoxing, I hadn't slept for eight days and nights and I didn't have my usual 'escape' mechanisms available. All I had all night every night was my Bible and prayer. I became so close to God.

That was the first time the Bible literally came alive off the page. It was so profound to me that at the end of that second week, I went into an ancient church alone, in the middle of the countryside (the rehab had allowed me out). That was the first time I gave myself to God one hundred percent. I was alone in the church praising my heart out, thanking him, tears streaming down my face with every emotion washing through me. It was an incredible moment. After a few minutes of praise, I felt like this massive *whoosh* move through my whole body. It's difficult to describe but it was this incredible *power* and *love*, better than any drug I'd ever done, and it was real. I now believe that this experience was me being filled with the Holy Spirit.

Later that day I went out again, for a walk in the beautiful countryside. As I was praying in gratitude I looked up and marvelled at this massive double rainbow that had appeared above my head. I have photos of both rainbows, from the time in Stroud before I went to rehab, and that day, after having been filled with the Holy Spirit. It was unforgettable, it felt so real and profound.

Back Home

When I got out of rehab weeks later, the love and support I had from my church was incredibly humbling and brought tears to my eyes. That first night, having a long, lonely drive back from Leicestershire thinking, 'What now? God help me!' I was driving back to a dirty, messy house. I opened the door and immediately saw my pastor and friends from church – Petros and Lucinda – had cleaned my house from top to bottom and packed the fridge with food. Words can't describe the love I felt. So blessed!

I was baptised six months later in April 2024. Since then, I've had what feels like an accelerated walk with the support of a mentor; prophetic words, gentle guidance and nudges to only look up to God for my healing. Deliverance was a large part of my walk during this year. I've lost count of how many evil spirits I've been delivered from, covenants broken and old traumas healed. Through the process of confession, repentance, forgiving others and myself, and asking Jesus to remove whatever dark spirit had been revealed. Writhing on my kitchen floor, crying my soul out and retching and throwing up all of this darkness that was inside me. Making sure that I prayed for the Holy Spirit to refill the gap left and praying Psalm 23 and worship music. I didn't want this stuff coming back.

I started experiencing the fruits of the Holy Spirit. My life-long anxiety is now mostly gone, which to me was an impossibility without those tablets. My depression is now mostly replaced with a peace and joy that I've never felt before. Everyone used to say I was the most impatient person they'd ever met but I'm now developing a patience that surprises me. I feel love, I cry at so many things. He truly is turning my heart of stone (stubbornness, resistance to God, and a lack of sensitivity) to one of flesh (responsiveness, obedience, and a willingness to follow God). There's a peace that I've never had before, and the green shoots of learning self-control for the first time in my life. It's a profound inner change and experience, and I am now very blessed in helping others on a path to Christ.

Reclaiming Relationships

In July 2024, Mum had a stroke. She was basically gone, out of it. This is when I first experienced the power of prayer for others. I started praying earnestly with her in the hospital (she's the first person I've prayed for and with), and the very next day she started her recovery, physically and in her spirit. A miracle! She's now absolutely fine physically but her memory is shot. But! She remembers the things of God.

In her own words she says prayer is literally the only thing that helps. Every time I see her we pray together. These are the most beautiful moments we've ever shared. It's absolutely mind-blowing as we've never had this spiritual connection before. I took her to church for the first time post-stroke recently and she cried with joy. She says that her last solid memory before the stroke is of my baptism and that it was one of the happiest days of her life.

For two months, while she was in the hospital, I prayed over her. Now she is able to pray for me, which is so beautiful. She says our prayer together is some of the most precious moments of her life which she'll never forget, and this is coming from a woman who possibly now has dementia. She thinks me being saved by Jesus is a miracle. The gratitude and joy I have for her being able to see my faith before she passes is beyond words. I didn't know before, but she said she had been praying for me for decades. Her biggest fear about me flirting with the darkness was that it was going to kill me, as it did my sister.

Hope

Being saved has not been a bed of roses by any means. No one shows you the small print. I thought I could now just put my feet up and relax for the rest of my life. But we are told to put on the whole armour of God because we are in an ongoing spiritual battle, not least in our own minds. We are to stand against the attacks of the enemy.

> 'For we do not wrestle against flesh and blood, but against the rulers, against the authorities, against the cosmic powers over this present darkness, against the spiritual forces of evil in heavenly places.' (Ephesians 6:12 ESV)

I'm starting to learn to stand in him. I do believe that since being saved I've had some spiritual attacks, and what's really helped with that is knowing my identity as a son of God, resisting the devil so he flees. God says that in our weakness he is strong.

I now have a hope I never had before. It is in Jesus, and after so many years of searching for truth, I now know *absolute truth*. By definition there can only be one. Jesus is the way, the truth and the life, and the only way to the Father. With God for you, who can be against you?

Lucinda's Story

I was stuck in what seemed like an abyss of endless emotional agony. Trauma rooted in my childhood had 'adrenalised' my whole nervous system. This, coupled with the chronic stress of the demands of parenting an explosive child, had created a storm in me; a maelstrom I struggled to contain. I would often find myself in my car, parked up in a lay-by, wailing, alone, in complete and utter emotional torment. It was during one of these times that I first put words to this pain; a desperate cry for help of some sort.

Soon after this my cry for help was answered in the most wonderful way, but I'll come back to all that later. For now, back to the beginning ... I grew up in an atheist family with my only church experiences being school harvest festivals and nativity services, with a sprinkling of weddings and funerals.

I was an anxious, sensitive child, and an easy target for bullying. The girl flavour of bullying: exclusion, rejection, whispering, name calling and note passing.

This created in me a real fear of people, and a habit that took decades to shift, of choosing the wrong friends. I dragged a heavy weight with me, of always feeling like an outsider.

I left home at almost eighteen and moved into a shared house in the nearest city, where I dived headlong into working hard and playing hard, ending up in a high-pressure sales job with materialistic goals and aspirations. The whole of my twenties was an unconscious quest to fill the emptiness I felt, through hedonism: feckless men, debauchery, recreational drugs and alcohol, alongside materialistic endeavours like clothes, cars and homes.

Becoming a Mum

That chapter of my life ended when I got married and had children, although that brought with it a host of new and intense challenges. My son arrived in the world after a traumatic delivery and he pretty much screamed from when he was half-a-day old until around six months of age. On one of the first few days after his arrival I had an experience of love flowing out of my heart towards him, and with this love came many thoughts of what I wanted to do for him; to support him and love him unconditionally. It was then that some of the frozen armour around my heart melted and I experienced love in a way I had previously not experienced.

I remember that the only time he was settled and not crying seemed to be when he was sucking a dummy while sitting in his car seat when I was driving. Although the first few years of his life were really stressful, it wasn't until I had a second child, a daughter, combined with moving house then renovating and extending that home, that I hit the wall and it all became too much. I experienced the first of two breakdowns.

Searching for Healing

This first breakdown was pretty mild. I had the sudden realisation of my 'issues', everything that was hidden in my subconscious came to the surface. I saw all the dysfunctional thinking that I'd lived with, not knowing any different. How I thought about myself, how I had such self-contempt and had taken on so much negativity about myself.

This breakdown was also the gateway into the New Age movement. Not that I would have called myself a New Ager during that time at all, not many people who are in that world really do. A need for healing is very commonly the doorway, and there are a myriad of different entry points. For me it was a combination of training in life coaching and reading *The Power of Now* by Eckart Tolle and then combining the two; I became a spiritual life coach. My focus was on 'presence' and 'consciousness' work, both personally and professionally rather than spiritual in the 'realm' kind of way, although I did work pretty hard at trying to cross into different realms. I wanted my own spirit guides, and I did enough shamanic journeys, but I was never successful, which I am now very grateful for.

My work was very focused on healing emotional wounds, which is something many people need, and although *some* of the tools in my tool box were helpful in a top-level way, what I was offering people was ultimately empty, as it was *self* focused.

Soon after entering the New Age movement I experienced around a year of a spiritual high. My son went to school, which gave my nervous system a much-needed break, my business was starting to take off and I ran a successful Facebook group for 'conscious mamas' who were working on healing themselves through their motherhood journey. My husband had also taken a six-month sabbatical to focus on his health, which had taken a battering from the high-stress home environment. In New Age terminology, I was in a period of ascension!

This 'high' abruptly ended when a few factors combined: my husband went back to work, the school holidays started, and I chose to become Reiki attuned. I had gone from struggling big time as a stay-at-home mum with two young children, to an environment of both parents around with just our daughter who was three at the time – two adults to one child – which was a pretty low-demand structure, back to just me with both the children and the constant explosions. It was a shock to my system and I spiralled. I also don't think it is a coincidence this happened at the time of becoming Reiki attuned and opening up myself to the spiritual realm. I remember on the Reiki course being so exhausted that I just wanted to lie down and sleep.

Falling into a Pit

This is when things got really dark for me. I had struggled with the burdens of motherhood before but this was another level. The depletion had me on the floor, figuratively and literally. It was like a tsunami of trauma swept me off my feet. Trauma from my childhood that had been previously repressed became unlocked and alive, combined with the intensity of the demands of motherhood while I was struggling. It breaks my heart looking back, not so much for me but for my children as they will have been greatly affected for the almost three years I was ill.

I didn't have enough capacity for myself, I certainly didn't have enough for them. Their emotional needs would not have been fully met during this period of time, and as much as I have tried to compensate for that since, it still breaks my mama heart.

I was struggling with the combination of old trauma, long-term chronic stress and chronic fatigue. These things put my nervous system on fire for a sustained period. The stress response can be different with different people and at different times, with the options being fight, flight, freeze or fawn. My reactions were all three except freeze. Fawn is where you fawn over others, trying to micromanage the situation to reduce the stress and protect others. This is a very common response for mothers of children. I would often be flooded with adrenaline and stuck in the fight response, my blood pumping with nowhere to release the burden. I wrote this poem while in the depths of despair of being needed by my young children while being chronically stuck in fight/flight stress response whilst completely depleted.

Intense guilt spiral
Need to escape
My sanity is dissolving at the edges
The little beings know, they feel it
Starving creatures, intensely clinging
They sense my heart is closing to us all
I've nothing to give
No crumbs for you or me
Fingers in my brain
In my heart
Feasting on me
I'm screaming inside
The crazy woman is clawing to come out
I hold her in with all my strength
As I know the guilt of her release is exquisite pain
Can't let it out
Can't keep it in

Seeking Healing

None of the New Age practices I had previously
leaned on had much of an effect. They were like tiny
plasters on a cavernous wound. I was a broken mess,
a puddle of despair. I saw no way out. Twice I drew
on the little inner spark of resource I had to arrange
a retreat: once at a friend's house for ten days
and one on my own in Glastonbury staying at an
ashram. During these two self-created retreats, I tried
various New Age practices to try to heal myself. From
conscious dance in a round house in the woods, to a
binding ceremony where I was wrapped tightly in strips
of fabric, mimicking an indigenous closing the bones
post-birth ceremony. From going through a rebirthing
process replete with being in a foetal position
surrounded by red cushions and blankets, to singing
mantras at a Hindu kirtan ceremony in the ashram.
I mean, I really did try all sorts during these combined
three weeks, and this is only a sample of the things I
did to try and recover my physical and mental health.

I did feel better during these retreats but I think that
was more due to the fact I had a break from the stressful
home environment. Both times when I returned home
it didn't last. During these almost three years I had
periods of being almost okay and periods of being in
the darkest pit (like the poem). But no matter what
I tried I could not get myself fully out of the hole
of brokenness.

Oftentimes, after a high-stress car journey, I would drop the family back home and just drive, alone, to decompress. I would drive and drive and cry and cry to release the tears and the stress. I would often pull into country lane lay-bys in complete and utter emotional agony. 'Help me!' was the cry of my heart and I spoke this out loud in my inner desperation. It's only with hindsight that I can identify this moment as a prayer. Back then I didn't imagine anyone was listening, least of all God. It was sometime in April 2018 that I heard a reply.

My 'Divine Intervention'

I was driving with both of my children in the back of the car and I had a sequence of thoughts appear in my mind; thoughts that were not *my* thoughts. This experience is pretty hard to describe but I will try. The thoughts were very subtle but also very strong at the same time and completely unconnected to my own thoughts. It was as though they were dropped in from outside of myself. At the time I knew this was a supernatural experience and called it my *divine intervention*. I had had a lifetime of anti-Christ conditioning from family, friends and the world at large, which is not unusual in this post-Christian era so it never entered my mind that this was God speaking to me.

The thoughts were, 'You have a house, you have a motorhome, rent out the house and go travelling.' It was like a light went on and a possibility of a way out of the pit I was in appeared. The pit I was unable to climb out of regardless of the New Age tools in my tool box, or by using my natural resilience and determination. I immediately mooted this to my children in the back of the car and they liked the idea (although I'm not sure they really understood the magnitude of the decision's impact on their lives). When my husband was back from work that evening I shared it with him and, as I expected, he agreed in a matter of seconds. I became energised and began selling our things, finding tenants for our house and arranging pet-sitting opportunities, and within six weeks we were off on an adventure. The adventure was just beginning.

We spent five months travelling around the UK while pet-sitting, but although this was fun and educational for our children they needed some stability. I had found out about a place in southern Spain which was a kind of hub for world schoolers (home education while travelling the world) and we made our way there. When I arrived I thought, 'How great, everyone is into the same things as me: women's circles, conscious dance, meditation, aka New Age!' We spent almost two years there and it was a very healing time; the sun, the sea, the community – which all helped to knit my nervous system back together and fill up my depleted soul.

From One New Age Hub to Another

This sunshine sabbatical ended soon after the first Covid lockdown in Spain came to an end. We decided to return to the UK, which we did in the summer of 2020. We ended up in Stroud, one of the most New Age towns in the UK, and I had the same thought, 'How great, everyone is into the same things as me: women's circles, conscious dance, meditation.' This time, however, I was pulled out of the spiritual darkness *masquerading as light* very soon after.

That next year, 2021, was akin to turning around an articulated lorry – from following New Age spirituality to following Jesus. The first seed that was planted was my concern about the 'Covid vaccine passport'. I could see the potential of it turning into a kind of tech fascism if it became entrenched in society. I saw Christians online saying this vaccine passport could be the 'mark of the beast'. This piqued an interest in me and at some point I bought a Bible. Parallel to this, I had also been discovering about the evil in the world, and that there are in fact Satanists who do horrifying things.

A day that sticks out in my memory was a Saturday in the February of that year. During my time in the New Age I had tried to break through into the spiritual realm, and although I had many friends who did converse with spiritual entities (aka demons!) I never managed to. On this cold Saturday I was driving along and in the near distance up ahead was a mass of black smoke moving from trees on the left, across the road in front of me, to trees on the right. I instinctively knew this was dark, not just in colour but in intention. It wasn't smoke from a fire, it was moving purposefully and I could tell it had a consciousness. It was a few metres by a few metres. This experience confirmed with me that the spirit realm is indeed real whereas before my belief was second-hand.

Over the next few months I heard the name of Jesus whispered around me, it was as though the name Jesus was being dropped into my mind. I also started to see that my spiritual worldview was the same, at its root, as satanic beliefs. The New Age world I had been in for seven years started to crumble as the veil was lifted from my eyes. I realised that if spiritual evil is real then spiritual good must also be real and became open to what that could be.

A Supernatural Gift

I was watching a 'Truther' video that brought together much of what I had learnt about the dangers of the New Age, and about the enemies of Jesus. At one point towards the end of this video I just knew, unmistakably, that Jesus *is* who he says he is in the Bible, that the biblical Jesus *is* the truth. It wasn't particularly anything on the actual video, just that the jigsaw pieces that had been in my head suddenly all came together and with that came clarity. At that point I hadn't really read any of the Bible or even heard the gospel, so I know this was indeed a supernatural gift.

I slowly started to read my Bible, to pray, and met more people online who were going through the same realisations. The next few months are a bit of a blur but the one moment that was very powerful for me was when I finally cried out to God in full confession. I would say sorry for things and ask for forgiveness during prayers but had never tackled my sin issue as a whole. I knew I wanted to have privacy for this, and with a husband who works from home and two children we were home educating, time alone at home was scarce to come by.

Finally, one Saturday evening I had my opportunity. On my knees it all spilled out of me, the burden of my life of sin was upon me, and the realisation that I had rebelled for the first forty-five years of my life. That my life, especially pre-motherhood, had been filled with defilement, debauchery and being led by my flesh, and that post-motherhood it had been filled with spiritual sin. All of the things I had done, the thoughts I had thought, the attitudes I had held – I laid it all out before God with tears streaming down my face. I then heard in my mind and my spirit, 'You are my child.' I knew it didn't come from me because at that stage of my journey I had not yet come to the realisation that God is our Father, so I know my mind wouldn't have thought this thought. It's quite hard to describe as it was such a fleeting moment but it certainly made an impact on me.

Soon after, I realised how similar this experience was to my first encounter with God, the time in the car that I had previously called my *divine intervention*. When God had come and rescued me even though I was in outright spiritual rebellion. Remembering this moment still opens my heart and my eyes start to leak, even now. The realisation is still so fresh that he came for me while I was utterly broken and desperate, that he saw my pain and distress and gave me the gift of a life raft, and I want it to continue to stay fresh for the rest of my days.

It took three years from his rescue operation to pull me out of the pit, to that Saturday evening on my knees crying out for his forgiveness on my bedroom floor. From despair to hope. From death to life. From bondage to freedom. From darkness to light. His glorious light. He saved me, literally in a multitude of ways.

I spent the first six months or so, including the moment of full confession of sin I just described, as a predominantly solo seeker of Jesus. I was praying and reading the Bible, and I had fellowship online to a certain extent but not in real life. Although I did talk to friends about Jesus and the dangers of the New Age quite a lot. I think that all of those early conversations have now come to fruition with those friends also now following Jesus. In this period of time I also started a Facebook group to share about the dangers of the New Age and help people cross 'the bridge' from the New Age to Jesus. As a life coach I was used to supporting people a few steps behind me, and I used this passion in a new way, to share Jesus. This Facebook group turned into a thriving community both online and off, with meet-ups, retreats and evangelism events.

Also during these first few months as a babe in Christ, the Holy Spirit cleansed me of many old pains and traumas. I would often find myself crying. But not gut-wrenching agony that produced tears of despair like in the pit. These tears felt holy and cleansing, as though God was crying with/for me. It was as though my heart was being gently tenderised; that all the places that held locked-away tears were being cared for as the tears were released. I would often find myself spontaneously singing thanks to Jesus in the car, the words would just appear.

Joining a Church

After six months I knew I needed to find a local church community, but not having grown up with any church background I had zero idea what to do or where to go. I was still suspicious of institutional power from my time down rabbit holes seeking truth. After a conversation with a friend who recommended a Baptist church – because in her words, 'they are quite biblical' – I went to the local Baptist church which happened to be Stroud Baptist Church. I asked Pastor Keith, when I first rocked up that morning, 'What do I do? I've not been to church before,' which he later told me had never happened in his forty years of ministry. That has been a relatively frequent occurrence since then as firstly my ex-New Age friends joined the church (two of whom have their testimonies in this book), followed by other new believers.

The first Sunday morning I attended church I had a little happy giggle with myself. It was a pretty old congregation and there I was, singing praise songs to Jesus with grandmas. What would my old 'New Age self' think, where 'spiritual glamour' and 'ego' was rife? This is the thing with the New Age mindset and worldview; it is marinated in pride, greed and spiritual superiority. It makes me shudder to think about what I used to believe. That I thought I could create my own reality. That I needed to deal with sin by 'integrating my shadow'. I was forever stuck in the future – when I get that thing, hit that goal or make that money, that is when I will feel contentment. When I reach an arbitrary level of success then I will be a 'good enough' person.

The world I had occupied was all about personal branding and greed, all about the image and not the substance. Selling or buying the dream, through people's pain points which is just so wrong to think of now. In fact, the world of personal development is symbiotic with the New Age, they are systems of spiritual consumerism. Everyone is buying, many people are also selling to the many seekers searching for healing. Once I do this next course, work with this coach/shaman, try this therapy, then I will be healed. Because that is what most people (at least the consumers) are there for; to heal physically or emotionally.

Transformation

Now I had received Jesus I was finally at peace, I felt true joy deep within me. I knew I had come home. All the broken pieces of me were mended and put back together. I finally felt whole and complete. What I had been searching for all those years was God. He was the One from whom complete healing came.

My Christian walk has not been a bed of roses. There was a very real spiritual battle both at the time of crossing the bridge from the New Age to Jesus, and afterwards. The waters can get choppy on the surface but the current underneath always has peace and joy. The pain, brokenness, self-contempt, 'never-enoughness', constant low-level anxiety, social anxiety and material grasping has been replaced with a lightness of being and deep contentment. It is well with my soul. I glimpsed this momentarily while in the New Age, as though behind a veil, but now I have seen and tasted that the Lord IS good.

The year I met Jesus I started a cleaning business. When I started it I had visions of building an empire and having other cleaners doing the actual work. But I ended up doing the cleaning for a couple of years which was vital for my walk following Jesus. If you'd told me I would be on my knees cleaning other people's toilets, I would have reeled in shock and disgust. *Me*, clean *other people's* toilets and dirt? No way, José, I would have thought. I am much too high and mighty for such degrading and menial work. But this time of cleaning was crucial and the timing was perfect. The gifts to my Christian walk were so precious; God moulded me through this work. He humbled me, to my knees, literally. Being in a position of servitude, serving, washing feet in a way, shifted my heart 180 degrees during the first few years of my walk. From self-serving and ego, to servant and service. From the greedy, aspirational, materialistic and capitalistic to the meek, humble, lowly and genuinely loving. God refined me and used this to make me more like Jesus. Now I am not saying this to glorify myself in *any* way but to glorify what God has done in me.

Home Sweet Home

The other area of my life where God has changed me from the inside out is through my home. I had always used home as a security blanket and had a life goal of having a detached country cottage with a bit of land. Nothing hugely grand but this was always an aspiration and one I assumed, based on my success in my twenties, that wouldn't be too hard to attain. But life throws curveballs, in my case this includes motherhood and health issues as described in this chapter.

When we returned to the UK from Spain, we sold our home as I wanted a fresh start and to not go back to the village where I had struggled in the pit. We did this just as prices were starting to sky rocket, and we were left without much ability to get a mortgage due to being self-employed. Prices quickly went up and out of our price range. The home we sold was a large four-bed semi and now we could barely afford a small three-bed terrace. I spent almost eighteen months glued to the internet searching for a home for us to settle in after years of semi-nomadic existence. We looked at dozens of homes and lost out on every home we made an offer for locally.

One home always stood out to me though, and felt like the one that got away. A sweet, dinky 1960s semi needing complete renovation, with a huge wild wrap-around garden bordered by a stream. The open day was busy and offers flowed in. As I expected, we were not successful with our bid. However, with God all things are possible. Twice I got a nudge through my thoughts (a bit like the other times) to email the agent and to let her know we were still interested if for any reason the sale fell through. During this time I also bought a lovely book filled with beautiful artwork made up of Bible passages, and while looking at one particular picture the words 'I am making a way in the wilderness' jumped out at me, which was next to a picture of a little pink cottage.

It turned out God was doing exactly that, as one morning soon after, I got a call from the agent and, without going into the minutiae, we secured the house for a more affordable price and could therefore buy it, which we did. We are still in the process of taming the wild garden but the house is now a home, our home, and I couldn't be more grateful. The old me would have had a chip on my shoulder about its size, whereas now I am so content with our little home.

In the New Age, people, as I did, 'work' at gratitude with daily gratitude practices, whereas now I *am* grateful. I don't have to 'do' anything. I am grateful to the One who made me, who sustains my life, gives me the breath in my lungs, who made a way in the wilderness and put my feet on the solid rock of his Word. I am free, in this home where I am typing this, looking out of the window onto trees coming into blossom, with the Lord's joy which is my strength and his peace that surpasses all understanding.

'Ask and it will be given to you; seek and you will find; knock and the door will be opened to you. For everyone who asks receives; the one who seeks finds; and to the one who knocks, the door will be opened.' (Matthew 7:7-8)

Amber's Story

Three years ago my life was turned completely upside down. I thought I had life figured out, until the veil slipped and I was struck by the realisation that I was completely and utterly wrong about the most important things. It hurt. I didn't want to believe it. But once I saw the truth, I couldn't unsee it. For once my eyes had been opened, I couldn't close them again and pretend everything was okay in the dark. It would be living a lie, and I believe we are destined for more than sleepwalking through life, living out untruths. I have always had a drive within me for the genuine and real, even when it's unpopular. So rather than accepting the comforting lies, I chose the truth that set me free.

I used to 'manifest my reality', follow the 'law of attraction', and readily consume astrology and channelled updates from various spiritual teachers. I used a pendulum to communicate with the spirit world. I became a Reiki master and pursued other energetic healing modalities. I had many crystals that I charged in the light of the full moon, and was constantly searching for more to acquire to protect and bring healing. I believed in reincarnation and did past-life regressions in order to bring forth memories of other lives. I believed in ascension from a three-dimensional world to a five-dimensional one. I thought there were many paths to God and that God was the universe.

All of my prior belief system was turned on its head in March 2022 when I came back to my Christian faith. This narrow path has turned out to be the way for me, in spite of how humble or unattractive it may seem to a world preoccupied with self and the temporal. This is my story of the love of God for me and my love for him. A story of a journey filled with broken wells that could never fulfil me. Yet first, I would like to start at the beginning, as all good stories do.

Early Years and Childhood

I grew up in a Christian home. My father was a youth leader, and from my early years I remember attending church services regularly. The church was a big part of my life and our broader community. I came to believe in Jesus at a young age, and was baptised as a teenager. I was passionate about my faith, but struggled with ways in which some professing Christians' actions didn't match up to their teachings about God.

I was shy and reserved as a teenager, and wasn't sure at all what I wanted to do with my life. I did know I wanted to help others, and went to college to pursue social work. I ended up switching career paths by completing a Master's degree in education, and became a public school teacher. My husband and I married, and eventually church became a background aspect of our lives as we became busy with the demands of life and small children.

I was a 'lukewarm' Christian and rarely attended church services or read my Bible. It wasn't that I didn't believe in Jesus or God, but faith wasn't a central focus of my life. With having my children, I became increasingly interested in holistic health and wellness modalities. I also became aware of world agendas but felt powerless to address larger macro-level deceptions and problems. As I became more into holistic health, I incorporated some things like hypnotherapy into my life but wasn't really looking for much spiritual exploration outside of Christianity.

A New Chapter and Hardships

My husband and I had bought a home near the elementary school I worked at, and lived there for five years. After having my son, I did not return to work and chose to stay home with him. We struggled to get by financially without my income and decided to sell our home and move to a rental near my husband's new job. This change made me feel a bit upended, but I made new friends and grew to love our new community. During this time, I worked at a private Waldorf Steiner school as an assistant teacher. My children attended the school as well. I felt a renewed purpose with my work. I didn't really delve into the spiritual world much during this time in my life.

The tuition costs were a lot the second year I worked at the school, as my toddler daughter began to attend. My first year working there, my in-laws had provided childcare for my daughter. Additionally, my son was having some struggles, and I suddenly felt called to leave the position I had worked so hard to obtain. During this time, we also decided to begin house hunting again, and almost bought a home. We did not complete the purchase due to concerns about our budget and our children's health.

This was a time of confusion in many ways – my job, our children's education, our home and our future. My husband and I prayed about our choices, before deciding not to go through with the home purchase. I felt a lot of fear and uncertainty about the situation. Additionally, the apartment we were living in had mould issues that were impacting our family's health. We backed out of the home purchase in October and I left my position at the school in December 2019.

During my time teaching, I had been given some crystals by co-workers, and began collecting others from a nearby metaphysical shop. I also occasionally took yoga classes and took my children to them as well, but wasn't deeply into the practice on a spiritual level. I kind of had one foot in two different worlds for a while. I remember when the pandemic hit, I started to listen to Christian music for the first time in a long time. It brought me peace and comfort in the midst of a confusing and isolating time.

Hopelessness and Spiritual Searching

In November 2020 we moved out of our apartment and into my in-laws' home. I was very upset about the move but our apartment was no longer a good fit for our family. It made financial and logistical sense, yet I felt like I was leaving the first real community I had found as a mother. In the midst of the move, I found hope in the fact that we were considering buying another home. However, that didn't work out and I found myself sinking deeper and deeper into hopelessness and depression as winter progressed.

In early spring of the following year I made a new friend online who ran a social media group on spirituality. I distinctly remember the first day I reached out to her. I had already participated in the group, where she told me the colour of my aura. Now I was private messaging her to find out more about my Human Design profile. I felt a sense of caution, like this wasn't a good thing I was jumping into. Yet, I ignored the feeling and forged ahead anyway. She became a friend and guru to me, as I frequently turned to her for advice and recommendations on all things spiritual. I quickly became well versed in Human Design and astrology, and listened to many spiritual teachers updates on astrology, as well as channelled messages and teachings on how to awaken my psychic abilities. I began reading spiritual books recommended by friends, amongst them: *The Four Agreements*, *The Celestine Prophecy* and *You're Not Dying You're Just Waking Up*.

I became obsessed with crystals, in my pursuit of protection and healing. I kept an ongoing list of what crystals I had and which I wanted to buy. I felt like I was never satisfied in my collection and was constantly looking to acquire more. I had several books that explained the spiritual meanings of the crystals, as well as how to clean and charge them. I began to charge them in the light of the full moon. I had a necklace custom made that included many different crystals for purposes I felt were needed in my life. I also bought a moldavite pendant, and wore both of these necklaces daily. Additionally, I had been given some amulets and wore them as well. I felt these things helped my healing and overall well-being.

My pursuit of all things spiritual continued to snowball as the year progressed. I bought Tibetan flags that represented each of the chakras, and hung them over my bed. I was following many New Age teachers and groups and sometimes asked people for psychic advice or to pull Tarot cards for me. I bought a pendulum and learnt to use it to communicate with the spiritual world, thinking I was talking to my higher self or others' higher selves. I attended a yoga retreat complete with a shamanic journey and created a mala bead bracelet. I learnt energy healing through several modalities. I began learning the 'Body Code' as well as Reiki. I took Reiki courses and became 'attuned'. I became a Reiki master and practised on myself, my children and several friends. When doing Reiki, I would see colours and images of spirit animals and chakras. I believed that I was helping others and had plans to open my own Reiki healing business one day.

My beliefs began to change as I immersed myself in these practices. I now believed in reincarnation, and participated in a group past-life regression. During this regression, I remembered a past-life memory and a memory from my own life for each chakra. These memories felt very real and were very emotional. I had past-life memories of being a young native American woman, a Tibetan monk, the wife of a sailor, a teenage boy who died of alcohol poisoning, a wrongfully imprisoned man, a middle-aged woman who committed suicide, and others. The true 'test' for me of these reincarnation beliefs was my *Titanic* past life. I had always been very interested in the *Titanic* and felt this must be because I had a past life where I travelled on the *Titanic*, and likely died in its tragic sinking.

I contacted a woman who offered to look into the Akashic records for me to see if I had a *Titanic* past life. For those unaware, the Akashic records is believed to be a large library containing all the lives lived by all souls and every event that has ever occurred or had intention for its occurrence. She told me some details about this particular past life, but she didn't know all of the information so recommended I try to regress myself to find out more. She told me I was on my honeymoon and was a second-class passenger. She wasn't sure of my name or my husband's. She also told me my soul came from an oversoul that was an aloe plant. She said hers came from an oversoul that was a snowflake. She said when we died, our souls went back to the oversoul and then could reincarnate after that.

I did a past-life regression on myself seeking to find out details of this past life. I used a YouTube video in order to do so. I saw the Akashic library and saw myself opening the book that contained this past life. I saw myself as this woman, with my husband, strolling on the deck of the ship. I pushed hair out of his eyes and behind his ear, tenderly. I seemed to know that his name was John, and that I had given him a pocket watch as a wedding present.

I did not allow myself to look up details of passengers until after completing this regression on myself as I didn't want to plant any ideas in my subconscious ahead of time. I was able to match my regression details with a real-life couple who perished in the *Titanic* sinking. I discovered the husband was found with the watch on his body; the wife's body was never identified, if it was recovered. This convinced me that reincarnation was real as I had 'proven' it to myself through this test. I told several of my friends all about finding my *Titanic* past life.

I also continued to dive into 'Truther' content about world events, and believed that the existing world was going to collapse in order to bring about a new and better world. This belief brought me a lot of spiritual pride. I believed I was transitioning from the three-dimensional world into being a more enlightened and ascended being, through going through four-and five-dimensional changes. I considered those who were asleep to world agendas and spiritual awakening to be stuck in the third-dimension. The teachers I followed explained that some people would not be able to ascend to the five-dimensional world and would not be needed. These individuals would pass away if they were not able to ascend.

I began eating a vegetarian diet as I believed that eating meat was low dimensional, due to the suffering of the animals. I was considering transitioning to veganism as well. I also began trading coffee for tea for 'dimensional' reasons. Protecting my energy and ascension were my main goals and I completed a number of practices regularly. These included spell work and 'codes', protecting my aura with rituals when going out in public, manifesting my goals through the law of attraction and cleansing my family lineage of blockages using the Body Code and Emotion Code. I used a pendulum to choose homeopathic remedies, sought out my spirit guides, and continued using crystals for healing and protection. I regularly used Reiki healing, practised yoga and meditated to empty my mind.

I also believed at this point in time that all religions or paths led to God, and readily shared these views with my friends. I had big questions for God, but rather than come to him with my questions, I made up my own answers or accepted those offered to me by others. I felt God and the 'universe' were the same thing. I no longer saw God as personal but more vague and detached from humanity. I never stopped believing in Jesus, but in my new spiritual worldview he was viewed as a good teacher or ascended master rather than as my personal Saviour.

I spent a great deal of money, time, energy and emotional investment in these spiritual practices and modalities. In the end these things became like a hamster wheel, a litany of never-ending practices designed to bring peace and healing that never quite delivered on their promises. I did find some temporary peace or good feelings, but never a true depth of healing or long-lasting peace.

Worldviews Upended

Although I was perfectly happy with my current belief system, a couple of things happened around the same time, in a way that could only be explained through divine intervention. Jesus came for me, in spite of myself.

A friend cautioned me about using the pendulum, as she had a close friend who had been 'psychically attacked' (a demonic or dark spirit attacked her) while using it. I began to notice a dark presence in my home. My daughter was filled with fear and had nightmares often, something that had not happened before. I began to see that there was a dark side to the spiritual playground I had dived head first into.

I followed a woman online, named Kate, whom I now consider a friend. She also has a chapter in this book. She wrote about 3D/5D consciousness as well as world events. She had a piercing way of shining light on dark places. I respected her perspective and I really enjoyed her writing. Soon I began to notice a shift in her writing, as she shared that she had found Jesus and was reading the Bible. I thought to myself, 'I already know this,' but something within me was drawn in with curiosity to her journey. She posted about The Bridge, a group on Facebook for those coming out of New Age spirituality and seeking out Christ.

I felt compelled to join, and as I made my first post I was instantly convicted, deeply within my heart. It was like the truth crashed into me like a tidal wave, and every belief I had held onto so tightly was upended. While all these things were taking place, I had also been hearing whispers from God in my spirit, thoughts that were not my own, that didn't fit within my current beliefs or worldview. I realised that Jesus was the only way to an intimate relationship with God, as the Holy Spirit spoke to my heart his words: 'I am the way and the truth and the life. No one comes to the Father except through me' (John 14:6). I had grown up in the church and never stopped believing in Jesus, but had been trying to mix New Age/New Thought spirituality and Christian mysticism with my faith. I had a sudden realisation that true Christianity and the New Age were diametrically opposed to one another and could not be reconciled.

My Tibetan chakra flags, which I had loved so much, now felt dark over my bed. I saw things for what they really were and not what I wished them to be. I saw the superficiality, the consumerism, the pride, and the works-based nature of New Age spirituality for the first time with unveiled eyes. Furthermore, as I looked into Theosophy, and the origins of the New Age in the West, I realised that I had unknowingly joined the religion of the 'elites', a group I would never have imagined joining willingly.

I came to a realisation of the truth that we only have one life on this earth, and then eternity after that. I do believe that some of my past-life 'memories' were of real people's lives, they just weren't mine. There are spiritual beings that have been around since the creation of the world, and can observe us, our lives and our relationships. These spirits can share this information with us if we open ourselves or our homes and families to them.

I realised that gratitude isn't a means to an end and 'manifesting' is not the same thing as prayer. God is God, and is sovereign over all, and I am not. I now come to him with humble requests, believing in faith but asking that his will be done, not mine. For he knows better than I what I need, as he sees the complete picture, and I do not.

I no longer believe the spiritual practices and beliefs I used to hold are the truth. And beyond that, I no longer find them necessary. I don't believe they can come close to bringing the fulfilment that I have found in Christ, in abiding in a true relationship with my Creator – the maker of the universe. For me, these things were a pursuit of truth and I had to try them all (and more) on, in order to find out what I now believe to be true, what I deeply know within my spirit to be the way: the person of Jesus Christ.

I have seen how his love and peace has transformed my life and the lives of others I love. It's a peace that is so beautiful and all-consuming that nothing else compares. The incredible love that I have experienced since coming back to my faith and coming back to God, is a love that won't let me go. A love that's deeper and further reaching than anything else I have ever experienced in this life.

I'm not ashamed to admit I am broken. I am a flawed human being who is still growing. I'd rather be authentic than try to appear perfect. I don't believe I can heal myself apart from my Creator. I have tried and it did not bring true healing or fulfilment. This isn't to say I don't accept myself. I have deep acceptance of myself and my path. Yet, I am now whole and complete in Christ, and it is so freeing and beautiful. He truly was the missing piece that holds all the parts of me together.

The story of Jesus has been twisted and misrepresented over time but at its heart, behind all the noise, is the simple truth of the gospel, the good news. The good news is this: there is a God who loved us so much he was willing to come and live in our mess and sacrifice himself for us. His love for us was so great that he left heaven to bridge the gap between our hearts and his.

This God encourages asking questions and searching for truth. He promises that if we draw near to him, he will draw near to us. There is no condemnation in him. There is love without measure or merit, peace that passes human understanding, and joy, true joy, that withstands any trial life may bring.

Since coming back to my faith, God has softened and humbled my heart in many ways – all glory to him, for I couldn't do it on my own. He began stripping away my people-pleasing nature and fear of being misunderstood by others. He taught me the difference between being nice and being kind, and showed me the value of authenticity.

He gently softened my heart when it was hard, surrounded by walls and broken. God gave me a sense of safety and peace when I was searching for shelter. He made me a home when I was a wanderer without roots. He promised to hold all things in his loving hands when I felt I had no control or autonomy. He gave me joy, despite the trials of life.

He showed me how to become love when I was focused only on myself and wallowing in self-pity. As I found wholeness in Jesus, he taught me to love myself and those around me. Now, there's no more need for striving, or searching for approval in others, as I am already loved completely and whole in his hands.

God has taught me to know him intimately and personally. No other spiritual experience compares to the heart-level knowing of being loved by God, fully, completely and wholly. Perhaps it seems paradoxical that freedom springs from surrender, but this is the way of Jesus.

I'd like to close with something I wrote about this journey, from the intoxication of the New Age and occult back to the sobriety of truth in Christ.

It was time to sober up.
The lies were so enchanting and captivating.
They felt so good and looked like the truth.
Yet the nagging feeling remained. Intuitively I knew something was 'off'.
The sobering truth cut through the intoxicating lies and got to the heart of the issue.

To my heart.
To continue in comforting platitudes would be
much easier than facing it.
But how could I be satisfied with pretending when
my heart knew the truth?
Waking up to my own ignorance was the hardest
thing I ever had to do.
All it took was a window.
A willingness to be wrong.
To fight the cognitive dissonance. Was I truly open-
minded? Did I know it all?
How humbling to find myself at the feet of
my Saviour.
Of the true God, not one of my own making.
Yet how freeing it was to surrender. To be free
from a beautiful and gilded cage that only
mimicked freedom.
The plot twist threw me.
It crashed over me like a tidal wave.
Oh, but how it made me whole!
So I abandoned my spiritual drunkenness for
living water.
It fills me up and has left me with a peace that
passes human understanding.
In it I've found hope that's held me and
won't let me go.
The truth can be a bitter pill to swallow when
you've been numbed and conditioned to exchange
the truth for lies.
But if you are willing to take it you may just find –
It sets you free.

'Jesus stood and said in a loud voice, "Let anyone who is thirsty come to me and drink. Whoever believes in me, as Scripture has said, rivers of living water will flow from within them."' (John 7:37-38)

'Although they claimed to be wise, they became fools, and exchanged the glory of the immortal God ... They exchanged the truth about God for a lie.' (Romans 1:22-23, 25)

Kate's Story

I didn't grow up in a Christian home, and I can remember my dad taking me to the local library one Saturday morning and showing me pictures of the evolution of man, from ape to human. The head of my primary school was an enthusiastic Christian who made us sing hymns every morning, even though we weren't a Christian school. I grew up with the idea that Christianity was something boring and that God wasn't real. There was a girl in my class who said she didn't believe in all that nonsense about how we came from monkeys. I thought how stupid she was, that my family knew better.

At age fourteen a lot of the pupils in my year at school started drinking. Alcohol was easy to get hold of as off-licences wouldn't check our age, or we would ask university students outside the shop to buy it for us.

After that, life was about friends, drinking, drugs, boyfriends, or casual encounters. It felt freeing after so many years at school being told what to do. Prior to this, from the ages of eight to thirteen I'd been friends with a group of girls who were more like bullies towards me. When this 'night time world' of older men, drink and drugs opened up, it was as if it felt like I could finally be one of the 'cool' people.

Chronic Fatigue and a Quest for Healing

When I was at university I developed chronic fatigue syndrome after a virus. I spent six months where I could barely leave the house and had to take a year out of my studies. I stopped drinking, as my system couldn't handle it anymore.

My life was simple and slow. I'd always loved writing and each morning I'd drink coffee and journal about my feelings. It helped me to feel good as I was so used to going out and seeing my friends, but now life seemed empty.

My mum had got into yoga and she recommended I try it. She told me that I could take one-to-one lessons and get a personalised yoga practice that could be designed to tackle certain health issues like low energy.

It was completely amazing, and after my first session I was filled with energy. I went out that night with friends without feeling tired, and felt hyper present in the moment. There was also an accompanying feeling that was quite strange as I also felt completely alone.

For three days I was in an altered state. The only way I could describe it is that it felt like I had set off on a path to enlightenment, and that I was separate from everyone. It was so lonely, and felt like a kind of drug trip.

From that first day onwards I did yoga every day, as it gave me energy. The strange altered-state feeling faded, and everything was 'normal' again. Except now I was a spiritual seeker. I gradually shifted away from doing yoga towards Tai Chi, which had similar benefits. I also started meditating.

When I went back to university, I still drank alcohol, but much more moderately. In my third year I developed a bad backache that made it hard to sit down for long periods. I tried going to a chiropractor, and while it helped put my back into alignment for a short while, the pain would always return. I had a friend who was off work with back pain. He was into meditation, and had been using a technique where he lay on his back and would focus on relaxing the pain.

I started trying it, and it worked. I could now sit for longer periods, and was able to control the muscles and relax them. Over the summer break I would meditate for really long sessions, sometimes twice a day. I borrowed books about meditation from the library so that I could learn more.

At the time I was in a casual relationship, and although I wanted it to be more serious, he was very non-committal. Like a lot of people of my generation, I had sex with my partners pretty early on in the relationship. One day I was having sex with him, and I had an orgasm that felt like a spiritual experience. It was as though a feeling of bliss came from outside of me and then into me. It didn't come from my own body, but from the spiritual realm. It left me in an altered state for the rest of the day, like I was stoned.

I'd had a similar experience once when my Tai Chi teacher gave me a hug. As he did so this energy went into me. On that occasion I also felt stoned for the rest of the day and when I asked him about it later, he said that he'd done it intentionally. I became fascinated by the spiritual realm.

After the summer I moved to Scotland for a postgraduate degree. I continued doing a lot of meditation and Tai Chi. I also started a part time job, and can remember it feeling pretty tiring at first. Whilst I had been cured of chronic fatigue and was able to lead a normal life, I struggled then, and still do now, with having less energy than the average person. I also tend to find it hard to shake off viruses.

One winter, the dark days started to get to me a bit. I began to have a kind of mental breakdown where I struggled to think clearly, and began feeling stressed by tiny things. At Christmas I started crying when everyone opened their presents on Christmas day and had no idea why.

I had always used writing to get through my mental upsets but this felt really different. I kept writing, and writing, but my mood didn't shift. I ended up taking three months off work as I couldn't cope.

During that period I met my now husband, Tony. While I still felt mentally unstable, we were so happy and in love. Gradually I felt better.

A Medical Procedure as a Doorway to the Spirit Realm

In April that year I had a gynaecological procedure called LLETZ for removing abnormal cells from the cervix. This is a very common procedure that happens after a smear test if they find abnormal cells that could turn to cancer in the future. I'd been told that the procedure was safe and minor, but it all felt very confusing, and scary. When I look back now, I think my body knew this was a big deal, but my conscious mind didn't.

After the procedure I developed major side effects. Physically my fatigue was back, and I could barely sit up without being in pain. I suffered major sexual dysfunction with complete loss of libido, pain during sex, and numbness, so if I had an orgasm I couldn't actually feel anything anymore. There were other really strange side effects like feeling disconnected from my physical body, and like I wasn't a sexual being anymore. If a couple were having sex on a TV show I would look at them as if they were aliens.

At the time I thought that I must be very sexually 'messed up' to have had major side effects from such a 'minor' procedure. I've since learnt, however, that there are thousands of women dealing with these major issues after going through the LLETZ procedure, as well as other secondary issues including post-traumatic stress disorder, early menopause, and many more.

I dived into learning about Tantra and spiritual sexuality, as I thought it could help heal me. I also continued to meditate regularly to try and deal with the side effects. I went to a Tantra workshop with Tony and had some blissful experiences that taught me it was still possible to feel pleasure, despite my broken body.

When I meditated I would either be focusing on counting my breathing or relaxing tension, however occasionally I got glimpses into the spiritual realm that fascinated me. One time I sensed the presence of a 'being' in the corner of the room. Another time, for a split second, I perceived time and space as disappearing. One day, I was very stressed and my husband's deceased 'father' (who I've never met), spoke to me and told me that I shouldn't worry and Tony and I should just be happy. I was amazed as until that point I thought that when we died we were just a mass of undifferentiated energy that joined together with other energy. I had no idea that people continued in a personal form, as a spirit (at least that's what I thought at the time, as I had no other explanation for this phenomenon).

That knowledge sent me deeper into learning about what happens after death, reading about near-death experiences and learning about reincarnation and past lives.

While I was happy being with Tony, I was not so happy living in Scotland. Since the dark winter when I got very depressed, I felt that I needed to go somewhere with better weather.

One evening I went to a meditation class. All my negative feelings about Scotland suddenly came to a head. I came home crying, telling Tony that I didn't want to live in Scotland anymore. He was actually quite up for an adventure. Slowly a plan came together. Tony works as a teacher and he had a friend of a friend working for an international school in Vietnam. This friend had written to us in an email about the rice paddies and karaoke bars, and it sounded so much fun. I thought of it as an adventure and that we would return home after a year or two.

Goodbye UK, Hello Adventure

In Vietnam I continued on my spiritual healing journey, going to yoga and meditation classes, writing about my feelings, and trying to learn about Tantra.

However, that was nearly impossible to figure out just from books. I longed to go to more Tantra workshops, but that sort of thing does not happen in Vietnam! Through a writing class I taught, I made friends with someone who was learning Theta healing – a kind of spiritual healing. I was her willing guinea pig. I'd try anything spiritual.

One January I was low in energy after a virus, but I wanted to shake it off so I went to a yoga class. Something strange happened in the class. I ended up with really painful legs and one of my legs had a lump in it. When I went to the doctor I was shocked when he told me that I needed to go and see a cardiologist. The lump was actually in my vein. When I went I found that the valves in both legs that make the blood flow back up my legs had stopped working. I've dealt with leg pain, varicose veins and circulatory issues ever since.

After four years we left Vietnam and moved to Switzerland. By this point I was feeling happier in myself, although not completely physically healed. In Switzerland we decided to have a child, as I had more vitality in the fresh air and healthy environment.

I had some health worries about the pregnancy but everything was okay. Apart from my decision to go to a pregnancy yoga class, after which I couldn't get out of bed for twenty-four hours. When I finally got out of bed and looked at my leg, I was horrified to see another zig-zaggy varicose vein on my leg. I got compression tights from my doctor and switched to Pilates.

Coming Into Agreement with the Occult

During my pregnancy I began to learn about psychic abilities after a writer I'd always loved wrote a book about training to be a psychic medium. I tried out some of the techniques in her book and began to get little bits of psychic information. For example, one evening, while falling asleep, I got a picture of a tiny sliver of moon − I felt like this was to tell me my daughter would be born on the new moon, which she was. I had planned a home birth, but one night the words came into my mind, 'You will go to hospital but it will all be okay.' And that's exactly what happened.

I loved being a mum, and pregnancy, birth and breastfeeding, and that closeness did more for my physical healing after the LLETZ procedure, than any of the spiritual practices I did. I have since learnt that babies in the womb produce stem cells that help to heal the mother's body so it's in the best possible health for pregnancy, birth and motherhood. (God's amazing design!)

When my daughter was two my grandmother died, and I felt what I thought was her presence around me all the time for a year. The grief caused more physical exhaustion, and my daughter watched way too many episodes of Peppa Pig. I had started doing a lot of yoga nidra (yogic sleep), which is lying on the floor focusing on different parts of the body. It felt quite amazing at the time but every time I started it, I could feel what I thought was the presence of my grandmother. I could 'sense' her in empty chairs, and when I walked in the forest.

I started to visit psychics to see if my grandmother would speak to me. It was amazing how accurate she could be in some aspects, but some of the things she said didn't seem quite right. I also went to a breathwork class which lasted two days, and I cried the whole time and saw a vision where my grandmother came out of a tunnel and stayed with me for the entire workshop.

We ended up deciding to leave Switzerland when my husband's contract came to an end. It was a huge source of anxiety for me about where we would move to. I used to talk to my grandmother's presence, so I asked her, 'Where should we move to?' and she said, 'Florence, Italy.'

Two weeks later a job appeared for my husband to teach in a school in Florence. My grandmother had always loved Florence, and had Renaissance art on her walls. It was pretty amazing.

Six months after we moved to Italy, the Covid pandemic happened. I struggled during this time, as I felt like I had all these spiritual tools but couldn't use them. I just couldn't concentrate enough for meditation. It was as though I needed a spiritual perspective on what was going on, and Buddhists talking about being indifferent to circumstances just wasn't the answer I was looking for.

I always found that writing articles about whatever I was struggling with had helped me to learn more, so I wrote a Facebook post asking what gave people hope during that time. My friends started talking about the 'great awakening' and how we were all ascending into 5D consciousness. That while the lockdown was dark, it was all part of a process of a greater spiritual awakening.

I followed their recommendation of different psychics and astrologers on YouTube. I was also hearing stuff online about end times, and 'the mark of the beast'.

I ended up reading the book of Revelation and, although I couldn't understand it, it started me asking questions. The 144,000 from the twelve tribes of Israel jumped out at me because one of the psychics I was following was talking about the 144,000 starseeds (a belief that some spiritual people are alien/human hybrids who are here to help humanity 'ascend').

Quest for Truth

What was the truth? I began to ask a couple of the psychics, one of whom often shared Bible quotes. They had various answers, about the Bible not being literal, and so I kept being open to it. I thought that the Bible was something I could incorporate into my own spiritual thinking.

Then one day I decided to say the Lord's Prayer. I instantly felt the presence of God. At that very moment I knew that I had never met God until then. I'd had all sorts of blissful spiritual experiences, but this was like a complete 180-degree turn.

In the New Age 'god' is seen as just another word to describe the 'universe', 'source' or 'god consciousness'. However, I had spent thousands of hours connecting with the 'universe' and I had never ever met God.

I instantly knew that the God of the Bible was real.

I bought a Bible and tried to start reading it but I didn't know what I was doing. I had a King James Bible and started on page one: the Old Testament. I fell asleep every time I tried to read and found it boring (although I was quite amazed at how long people lived back then!) It probably sat on my bedside table for six months. Ever since my daughter was born I had always struggled to read at night as I didn't have much energy and would fall asleep instantly.

During this time I had friends online who were coming to similar realisations, who were also looking into the 'false light' of the New Age. We'd share resources and videos as we tried to figure it all out. I watched many 'New Age to Jesus' testimonies on YouTube. I listened to Doreen Virtue's testimony of being the number-one bestselling author in the New Age and then coming to Christ. She recommended the New Living Testament version of the Bible as being easier to read, and, at that point, a Christian friend told me to start reading with the book of Matthew in the New Testament. I found that was a lot easier.

At some point I must have been 'saved', but I don't remember an exact moment. At first I carried on doing yoga and meditation, as I wasn't sure what was wrong with them. Then I listened to a few testimonies of ex-yoga teachers. They were explaining how every pose is designed to worship Hindu gods. I stopped as I realised it was breaking the second commandment and worshipping other gods.

Through listening to testimonies, and reading the Bible, I learnt that there are no other gods, and the spirits we connected with are actually demonic. Through the videos created by a woman who used to be psychic and came to Christ, I realised that psychic mediums are not actually in communication with dead loved ones, but with demons 'masquerading as an angel of light'. This was a hard one to let go of for me, but as I read the Bible and understood how the spirit world worked, I realised that it is Satan and demons luring people into spiritual experiences that feel good but are actually demonic in nature. Reported past-life experiences also turned out to be deception by demons implanting false memories.

I continued with meditation for a while longer as I wasn't sure what was wrong with sitting in silence concentrating on my breathing. Dealing with fatigue I felt I really needed that stillness and rest time. Another ex-New Age friend mentioned it might be okay as long as we didn't open ourselves up as a 'portal', trying to channel spirit entities. However, I remembered that time I'd been meditating and sensed a being in the corner of the room. I hadn't been deliberately opening myself up as a portal then but it still happened.

Eventually I also gave up meditating when I realised I could get all of the benefits of stillness and relaxation through prayer. As I gave up these practices, I started to realise how much they are like addictions. I'd done my yoga every morning without fail as otherwise my head wouldn't feel clear for writing, and my body would feel tense, and desperate for exercise.

However, after coming to Christ I could go a few days without exercise, and just have a walk and do some gardening and it was fine. I've switched to some non-yoga stretches, online step or dance workouts, and having a dog. I still need to exercise, of course, but it's not like an addiction where I have to do it every day.

Looking back I can see the spiritual bondage that these practices put me under. Yoga cured my chronic fatigue dramatically, but it set me on a lifetime of spiritual seeking. Spending money on different workshops and courses, looking for a miracle I never found.

What I've realised is that yoga and meditation offer a short-term high, like a drug, having to keep going back for more and more, often going deeper and deeper to continue to get the high.

With something like Tantra, the spiritual sexual experiences can be intense, but they can bring emotional lows too. There are many reported cases of people who report blissful spiritual experiences but end up feeling emotionally numb on the days following. These practices are just like drugs, rather than having a genuine relationship with a God who helps us in our lives. It's worth noting that becoming a Christian has been better for my sex life than any spiritual sexual practice. I never thought I'd write that but it's true.

What is most deceptive about 'spiritual highs' is that we don't see the side effects, the spiritual warfare that opens up in our lives, when we literally do a deal with the devil. Looking back I realised the mental breakdown I had was likely caused by spending hours and hours meditating. It is dangerous exploring the spiritual realm outside of God.

I discovered there was a psychiatrist who worked near a meditation retreat centre. She got so many patients coming to her from the centre, that she decided to investigate the effects of meditation on mental health. Contrary to what we are told, meditation had a negative effect on the mental health of all the participants.

In another research study of school children who practised yoga and meditation, the children reported experiencing benefits that could not be objectively measured. I find this interesting as this is exactly what the New Age does – it gives you short-term spiritual highs to make you think you are feeling better, when actually, long term, it's making you feel worse.

The New Age is a complex labyrinth that leads you deeper and deeper, becoming more and more lost. There is always more 'inner work' to be done, and more money to be spent.

The Bible tells us to 'be alert and of sober mind' (1 Peter 5:8), whereas meditation and yoga are designed to cultivate a trance state. The act of meditation, where you practise seeing yourself as a neutral observer – watching your thoughts float past – in my opinion is a practice that severs us from the self, causing a disconnection that can open us up to demonic oppression.

The devil can 'heal', as my experience with yoga shows, but he will always demand a payment of some kind. My body is a testimony of what that payment can look like.

God still performs miracles today and I will continue to pray for my full and complete healing, but I also know that sometimes for the greater good that healing does not happen until heaven, when believers will be fully restored with new bodies.

As I write these words I think of the thousands of pounds I spent going down false avenues trying to heal 'self' with 'self', which can never work. We are born with a God-shaped hole inside of us, separated from him by our sin, and the only way to truly find peace is to reconcile our relationship with God through Jesus.

God came to me through prayer, and I do believe that anyone who seeks him with an open mind will find the truth. I believed because I felt his presence but now I love learning about how much evidence there is for the accuracy of the Bible and Jesus's life, death and resurrection.

I have a peace I never experienced before, and a weight has lifted from me. I never realised just how much unconscious guilt I carried with me because I rejected God and sinned against him.

I still struggle with low energy from time to time, but my energy is better than ever. I spent ten years unable to read a book before bed, but now I get excited to read my Bible every night, and actually stay awake! That is the power of God's Holy Spirit to make us a new creation.

One thing I've struggled with throughout my adult life is cooking and cleaning, and having the energy to keep a tidy house. I still do. But it is better than it has ever been because God is a God of order, and he's helping me get my life organised.

When I was in the New Age, I was constantly looking around for something bigger, the next course, the next spiritual high. Now I am happy with the simplicity of having a relationship with God through prayer and reading the Bible, and being with my family and church family and friends.

On one occasion I spent 100 euros to be given life guidance by a 'channeller'. She told me that I would need a lot of 'independence' in my marriage, because my husband did not understand me. That I had never been properly understood by anyone. The channeller told me that I too had a gift to be a channeller.

This is how Satan deceives, through flattery. He led me to crave more, to want more, and to think that what I had was not enough. I was left confused as I always felt my husband did understand me. Even so, there was a strange seed of doubt, as I naively trusted everything I heard from the spirit world. When I was in the New Age I had no spiritual discernment. I believed everything I was told by people in touch with the spiritual realm because I didn't realise that there are demonic spirits who lie. But the Bible tells us that Satan is 'the father of lies' (John 8:44).

As a spiritual being I deeply craved a relationship with my Creator, but I was looking in the wrong place. I saw the church as something boring, that it is just a controlling religion, rather than the truth. As I've been growing in my relationship with God, and with other believers, I have been excited to learn about the spiritual gifts; that God still speaks to people today, through dreams, visions and prophecy.

Some of the 'New Age to Jesus' testimonies are very dramatic with intense spiritual experiences. One day I actually prayed to God about this, as in comparison my journey to Jesus seemed tame. I can't remember the words of the prayer but God answered me later with an image in my mind of an overflowing cup. Then the words, 'My cup floweth over' came to me. I googled it and realised it was from the book of Psalms in the Bible. I'd never even realised at that point there were Psalms!

It has been amazing to build my relationship with God. It says in the book of James (4:8) that if you draw near to God, he will draw close to you.

Jackie's Story

Growing up was difficult. I had a very challenging relationship with my brother, who was eleven months older than me. We were always fighting and arguing, even as toddlers. One of my earliest memories is from when I was aged four when my brother threw me out of a moving car. I fell onto the road but was completely unharmed, which I truly believe was a miracle and that God protected me. I was highly sensitive to the spirit realm from a very young age and often felt the presence of scary entities around me.

Around age six, my brother started what he called a 'game'. He would put a pillow over my head to see how long I could last before I couldn't breathe. It was terrifying – I remember fighting for breath, although the memory itself is foggy. He would also strangle me and twist my neck while saying, 'We'll just do this to see how long before it really hurts.' These experiences left me deeply traumatised.

Throughout my childhood, I suffered from recurring nightmares — dark visions full of monsters that still haunt me today. Around the same time, I experienced sexual abuse. Two older boys exposed themselves and tried to force me into sexual acts. I didn't fully understand what was happening, but I knew it was wrong and felt overwhelming fear and shame.

Abandoned

When I was nine, my sixteen-year-old cousin came to live with us. She was very broken herself and exposed us to horror films and pornography. Then came the most devastating blow — my mother left to be with another man, divorcing my father. I begged her not to go, but she abandoned me and my brother with our dad.

After my mother left, our home stopped feeling like home. My father got a girlfriend and was never there. From age twelve, I essentially had to parent myself. Despite everything, I maintained some belief in God, though I didn't yet know Jesus.

The pain drove me to numb myself with solvent abuse, smoking marijuana, drinking and LSD. I was very lost and very lonely, crying myself to sleep each night, only to wake up terrified, convinced I saw spirit children watching me in the dark.

At fifteen I left Newcastle, my hometown, for Brighton, where I spent the next few years clubbing and partying. Yet there was always something in me that didn't want this life, because inside I remained deeply unhappy.

My string of abusive relationships continued when I met someone I thought loved me, but he turned out to be controlling and possessive. His jealousy grew into aggression, until one night he threw me down the stairs, and that was when I knew I had to leave. Desperate, I phoned my mum at 2am, begging her to come and get me until she reluctantly agreed.

At this point I was twenty years of age, and although it was a relief to have some kind of shelter living at my mum's in Hertfordshire, I remember looking out the window one evening and just thinking, this whole world isn't right. It felt like I could sense a negative atmosphere all around.

Just when I thought I could relax, I discovered I was pregnant. It was my worst nightmare, having a child on my own without solid family roots. I ended up speaking to my mum and her partner, and they encouraged me to get a termination. I do not blame them because I made that choice. It was the hardest thing, and it completely broke my heart as I didn't want to do it. I remember going to surgery, and I think I heard God's voice for the first time. He said, 'You don't have to do this.' I was so scared I thought I'd imagined it. I didn't realise how completely broken I was at that point of my life.

Marriage and Spirituality

Shortly after that I met the man who is now my husband. We would party together and have fun, but inside I was incredibly unhappy, and in desperation I took an overdose. I had a near-death experience and all I remember is feeling like I was in a big battle trying to defend myself. With hindsight, I think I was trying to defend my case with God. When I came back to life I knew I had to change.

I believe God had his hand on me, and my husband stayed by my side. I still had horrible depression that I battled and hid, chronic panic attacks that I couldn't hide and I would often collapse into self-hatred.

By that point my husband and I had a little place together. The office where I worked would sometimes have little stalls in the foyer and I was drawn to a crystal stall, and all the pretty colours. I started chatting to a lady who had one of the stalls. It was so easy to open up to her about my anxiety and depression. It was as if she knew things about me. Amazing, I thought. It was like the first glimmer of hope in my life.

'Have some Reiki,' she said. 'I've helped lots of people.'

I was so intrigued.

The first time I had Reiki, I instantly had a spiritual experience. I saw an amazing light which was like being kissed by an angel. Something was suddenly different and I had a moment of intense clarity. It was so brief, but it was enough to leave me wanting more.

In my Reiki sessions I'd lie there with my eyes shut and have amazing visions. One time she suggested we do some angel cards. She gave me a reading and started telling me I had a gift, that I was psychic. I thought, 'Wow, I have a superpower.'

After that it was like the doorway to the spirit realm was swung wide open. I kept hearing about spiritual events. I began reading books about angels and getting into all kinds of New Age things. A lot of it was helping me, and my anxiety reduced and my confidence grew.

Then I fell pregnant, but it was an ectopic pregnancy. I was devastated. It felt like I was being punished because of the abortion. I became desperate to know if I'd ever have a baby so I went to visit a psychic, who told me I was gifted. I became pregnant with my son and started learning to read Tarot and practise Reiki. One thing led to another and I moved onto spirit mediumship and I realised I could see all these spirits. This is it, I thought. I've found my calling.

There was one woman I met at a psychic circle who was a big name in the spiritual community. She told me, 'You're really special, you're different.' I remember sitting in her house and seeing dark spirits like goblins. 'I'll just ignore it,' I thought, and I decided to just focus on the good aspects. I had no idea what I was thinking!

I started a little business, having trained in massage, reflexology and then added Tarot and healing. I was still depressed and took guidance from my medium friend whose spirit guides told her I should go on antidepressants. I trusted them, and ended up being on them for over ten years. The drugs did give me some sense of relief even though I didn't feel fully better. They numbed my emotions and that made me a more useful channel for the spirits. My main focus was that I wanted to grow spiritually.

I really loved crystals, and ended up running a crystal shop because it increased my clients for spiritual readings and Reiki. I was building quite a name for myself and felt like I was a better person than in my partying drug-taking years. There was some good in the New Age, it was like a bit of truth mixed with a lot of lies.

Things Turn 'Dark'

After offering 'spiritual services' professionally for a few years, I started to see the dark spiritual entities again. When I was with certain clients I would perceive darkness around them. One day, a regular client came to see me. She was a lovely lady who I knew well. During the reading I remember looking at her, when all of a sudden I lost track of time, I felt drunk (despite not drinking), and I started slurring. What was going on? I needed this woman out, like immediately!

The next twenty-four hours after she left were absolutely awful. I felt lost, as if I was part in my body and part out of my body. It felt like there was someone else with me, another being, so I phoned a medium friend and asked her for help.

'You've got an attachment.'

'What?' I exclaimed.

She started swearing, telling this stuff to get away from me.

After she did this, I felt a massive sense of relief as if something had been lifted off me.

'Your spirit guides are training you,' she said.

'For what?'

'You're gifted. You're going to remove these horrible attachments from people. Loads of people have them.' She kept reassuring me saying, 'If you just shout and swear at them, they will leave you alone.'

After that I started going on what I called 'ghost-busts'. Entities would appear, and I'd start swearing at them. At one ghost-bust there was a horrible darkness and fear that overwhelmed me. It was like this darkness was following me everywhere. For days there was a black heaviness all around me. Then it started saying it wanted to kill my son. I freaked out, and started cleansing my house, sageing it and putting crystals everywhere. I shouted and swore at the entity saying, 'No, you're not having my son.'

The spiritual experiences were only intensifying by this point. My house was full of spirits or ghosts, which I believed were dead relatives. At one point I sensed a queue of them around my house. I sought advice from my spiritual friends and they said, 'Well, it's because you've got this gift. These spirits want to communicate through you. You're going to help people.'

Well, I thought, I don't want anyone to have these dark attachments. I'm happy to help them, if that's my calling.

I remember a male client contacting me who used to buy crystals from me. He phoned me up, wanting my help. 'Something dark is attacking me. My dogs are really sick,' he said. He told me he went to another crystal shop that had a lot of witchy and spell things in it. The lady who worked there said, 'We want to help you – can you come back when the shop shuts at five?' So he returned at five, and she pulled back a curtain at the back of the shop. There was a star with a circle in the middle, a pentagram, and she asked him to sit in the middle. Then she came out of the back with a gentleman, and they were both in robes. They took the robes off and were both naked, and when the man pulled out a knife, my client ran out of the shop.

He wanted my help as they had put a hex on him, a negative spell. This was all too much for me, so I passed him onto another medium. When I spoke to her later on, she told me to stay away from those kinds of shops, because they are involved in the underworld. I didn't really understand it all at this point.

I couldn't cope with this dark side, so I decided to stop dealing with 'attachments'. I told myself that if I just talked to the angels, then I'd be protected. So I started working with angels, and my experiences changed. Now all I saw were pretty colours, lovely orbs, fairies and butterflies. I started running angel courses and I was quite happy for a while.

I then decided to do the Reiki level-two qualification. The teacher was incorporating angels into the training and she was using the archangel Michael and other archangels. Immediately afterwards I felt euphoric. It felt like I had ascended to another level, spiritually speaking. But in the following days, I crashed and felt really depressed, sensing so much darkness around me again. Spiritual friends were saying, 'It's just your inner child. You can get a lot of emotional stuff coming up to process, so you can heal. You'll be alright.'

About a week or so later I was with two of my close friends who were also into spiritual stuff. They thought it might help to give me an angel card reading. My friend sat opposite me on a massage table in their dimly lit room. She gave me my reading, which seemed really accurate. Then I looked up at her – and I'll never forget this – this huge being was towering over her, the most solid spiritual being I'd ever seen. It had a face like a dragon, wings like a bat, and it was emanating terror. It started walking around the table.

'You're not talking to a spirit guide,' I said to her, and explained what I could see.

She looked suddenly angry. 'Jackie, these beings are here to help you.' My friends couldn't see what I was seeing.

I told myself, 'Don't let it know you're scared.' In my head I was swearing at it and telling it to go away. Then it disappeared. I made my excuses and left almost immediately.

After that my friends distanced themselves from me quite dramatically. I went through a three-month phase of just lying on my sofa, crying. I thought it must be a 'dark night of the soul', a spiritual concept I'd read about. In that way I could normalise what was happening.

Gradually I came out of it, and one of the things that helped me was learning about an idea called 'ascension'. I believed that spiritual people were shifting into a higher state of consciousness called 5D. I started following different spiritual gurus online. They were saying that the world was going through a spiritual transition, that we're purging the darkness out of the earth, and going through an 'ascension process'. I was determined to 'raise my vibration' and 'ascend to 5D'. I started doing courses about it and even went on to do my Reiki Master course.

False Light to True Light

My mood improved again, and I was coming off my antidepressants slowly. Then Covid hit. Something didn't seem right about the whole Covid thing and I was wary of the vaccinations and felt like there was something seriously wrong in the world. A friend kept showing me bits of information about deception in the world. Part of me didn't want to look at it as I thought the negativity would 'lower my vibration'. But I did look because I was trying to make sense of my perception that there was something really wrong with the world.

Meditation was a big part of my life at that point. I was off with the fairies, having out-of-body experiences. One day while I was meditating, my mind drifted to thoughts about the darkness in the world. Then I started worrying about my husband and son. What if they didn't 'raise their vibration'? What if they had to reincarnate and learn their lessons all over again? Then I heard this really peaceful voice, it was the most peaceful voice I've ever heard. 'Everything's going to change, your whole work, everything.' Wow, I thought, I must be going to the next level of my ascension.

After that things started to go wrong in my business, or what I perceived as wrong at the time. I started to feel unwell and depressed again. I think it was withdrawal from the antidepressants.

One day I was on a women's retreat. We were doing rituals with flowers, honouring and blessing each other. It was all about love and light, and being goddesses. But I remember looking round at everyone, and thinking they didn't look right. My Reiki Master teacher was there and at one point I saw this black thing in her eye. I thought it was my imagination. At that point I just wanted to get home.

After the retreat I started falling back into depression. I said to my guides, 'What do I do? I've got all these clients coming to see me.' They told me to go back on my tablets. So I phoned the doctor, and they agreed straight away. But this time they made me feel ill. I had pains in my stomach and struggled to get up. I had to cancel all my work. It was all so confusing.

There was one friend, Sally, who stuck with me throughout all my difficulties. She reassured me, 'It's all right, you'll get back on your feet.' Then a few days later Sally sent me a Facebook post from her Reiki teacher, saying that she had given her life to Jesus. I didn't understand what she meant. Sally sent me the Reiki teacher's testimony. I looked at the photo of this woman on her post and she looked like she'd stepped into another reality. It felt weird. I put blinkers on straight away and didn't want to know about it.

I started hearing voices saying to me, 'Kill yourself.'
Am I imagining it? I thought. I just need to meditate
and 'raise my vibration'. At this point I was in a
spiritual battle without even knowing it. Then, every
time I went on Instagram, there was an American
lady appearing on my feed talking about Jesus. She'd
had a massive spiritual business, but had a complete
turnaround. She was saying, 'These spirit guides aren't
who you think they are.'

Fear came over me. Part of me didn't want to hear it. The
lady said, 'Don't take my word for it, ask God yourself.' Is
this part of the ascension? I wondered. I was scared, and
feeling weirdly guilty. I sat down, and wrote out a prayer.

'God, please show me, am I doing anything wrong?'

Then I had three intense nights of dreams. The first
night, I dreamt I was walking through a cobbled street
and there was fire and smog everywhere. A man with
a staff approached me but I couldn't make out his
face as it was so dirty. He pointed the staff at me,
and it turned into two snakes. There were very dark
things happening around me. When I woke up, I tried
to reassure myself, 'Just meditate, raise your vibration.
It's just a dream.'

On the second night, I had a sense that God was
with me. He was in my heart. It's okay, I thought,
feeling better. The third night, I nearly flew out of
my bed. A thunderous voice bellowed, 'God is truth!'

It reverberated throughout my whole being, like my whole soul was shaking.

Over the space of a week, I managed to calm down and one day I sat and prayed, 'God, if you're real, you are going to have to do better than that. You have to show yourself.' The next day my friend Sally invited me to a Stand in the Park (anti-lockdown and compulsory vaccination protest) meeting, so I went along. This lovely couple came over to me, and we were talking about Covid. He said, 'You know, this is all part of Satan's plan. It's all going to be wrapped up like an old garment, Jesus is coming back soon.' What's he talking about Jesus for? I thought. Then he started giving me his testimony. He said, 'I was into Transcendental Meditation. I was doing Tarot...'

The couple were nearly seventy years old but he told me he had been walking with Jesus for forty years. 'So do you think angel cards are bad?' I asked him.

'Well,' he replied, 'they're not of God.' Then he started telling me that Jesus died on the cross for my sins. The next thing I knew I fell on the floor. I couldn't stop crying. 'Do you want us to pray for you?' he asked.

'Please, anything that will help me!' I sobbed.

They prayed for me, and Sally started praying too. It was funny as she'd just completed her Reiki level-two course, but here she was praying! After that, the couple needed to leave, but they gave me their number so we could keep in touch.

Immediately after they left, another woman approached me. She said, 'I'm a Christian, don't worry, God gave you those psychic gifts.' It was like the devil tried to get to me straight away, to get me off track.

A Battle

That night I slept surprisingly well, and the next day I took my dog out. Walking in the fields I could not stop crying. I was confessing all the things I had done wrong in my life, saying, 'Please, God, forgive all of us, have mercy on all of us. We're all evil, please forgive us.' Then everything was really noisy. It felt like I was being pulled from one side to the other, and I couldn't think straight. I shouted out, 'Will you just shut up, the lot of you!' Then it went quiet.

After that I went through a horrible two weeks. I couldn't eat and my hair was coming out. I knew then there was something not right with these spirit guides. I asked that they reveal themselves in the name of Jesus. Then they turned. I felt like they wanted to kill me. I was seeing horrible things, like a giant eye in the bedroom.

Then one night, I was under my blankets and I felt something so peaceful, a presence, like a man in the bedroom. He looked like he had a robe on him, but I was scared to look. I glanced at him quickly and then hid under my blanket. Whatever it was, I sensed his care and concern for me. I believe this was from God.

Then things got even more horrible and things intensified. I convinced myself it must be because I wasn't taking my medication and had psychosis, but it was a battle for my very soul. I went to stay with my mum for a week and I hardly spoke a word. I must have just been in shock, and I remember looking in the bathroom mirror and seeing this black inky thing move across my eye. I was just so terrified. I lay in bed repeating, 'Jesus Christ, help me,' and things would calm down. I told my mum what was happening and I think God started healing our relationship there and then. I would ask her about religion and she told me she was christened as a child. I remember her saying to me, 'Well, maybe we should have got you christened.' When she said that, a feeling of peace came over me.

After that I went on a crazy, thirteen-month journey. I thought, right, don't go near the spirit guides, just stick to the Reiki and pray. I don't know why I thought that would be okay after everything, but I did. But God is graceful and merciful and eventually I gave up Reiki too.

Every day I prayed, 'God, give me eyes to see and ears to hear.' He showed me the truth. He began to show me all the evil that is in the world, and I would come across posts and YouTube videos. I heard many testimonies and discovered the depths of satanic rituals with people in power, and all about dark levels of Freemasonry. It was one rabbit hole after another and it all pointed to Jesus as Saviour.

I met up with the wife from the couple in the park as I had questions. She was talking about Jesus and I felt this power coming at me. I wanted it, but I was scared. I thought, what if I say yes but it's wrong? I then went on a journey trying to disprove Jesus because I didn't want to be deceived again. But God kept showing me, 'No, I'm the truth. Jesus is the truth.'

A friend invited me to church where I met a lady. We were chatting and I mentioned Reiki. 'Reiki's not right,' she said to me. 'God wants you,' she continued.

I replied, 'Oh, I don't know if I like that.' It felt a bit scary. I went down to the front when they invited people to come for prayer. I fell to the floor from the power of the Holy Spirit. When I got up I started to feel nauseous. They were shutting up the church and this woman approached me and said, 'Do you want to have a chat outside?'

Freedom

I didn't know what was going on but she did. She started praying for me in the car park, and I started manifesting demons. I was on the floor, shuddering, and I felt a hand on the inside of me. It didn't want to let me go. The lady prayed and tried to cast this thing out of me. At this point it was clear to me that Jesus was real, but I sensed I hadn't been fully set free from the demons. I felt like there was still something there. I phoned the couple and they invited me over.

The day I was going there I felt a darkness creeping up on me. It didn't want me to go to the house. I was so nervous, wondering what I was doing. The couple were just casually chatting, as if I was normal. He asked if they could pray for me. Then I manifested demons again. Something inside of me was screaming, and I was screaming. Then something very evil came out of me.

Then they prayed again, and I felt a huge sense of peace. I knew then that Jesus *is real*. I didn't want any of the dark stuff anymore. I wanted to officially give my life to Jesus.

Next, I went on a whole journey of getting to know God, and being cleaned up from all the stuff I had done. I was becoming a new creation, it's just amazing. After my conversion, I went through a really difficult year of spiritual warfare, but through it I grew so close to Jesus.

Since then I've overcome the antidepressant withdrawal and God has healed my depression. I did go through some anxiety but God is so good, he just held me through all of that. I learnt how to get into his presence, and to stand on the truth of his Word. The old Jackie, my old life, it doesn't feel like me anymore. That Jackie died in the water when I got baptised.

Now I have so much joy. People comment on how I'm happy all the time. I was a positive person in the New Age, but some of it was a mask. This is a genuine joy in my inner being. Even when I'm going through spiritual warfare and fiery trials, I am still connected to a joy and peace that surpasses all understanding.

I'm a nicer person now too. Even though I've always had a passion for people and wanted to help them – the work I am in now is as a carer– the love God has placed in my heart for people and his love for them blows my mind.

'You will know the truth, and the truth will set you free.' (John 8:32)

Kat's Story

I was eighteen when I started to dabble in witchcraft. When I started university, there was a 'witchy' shop I used to go to and buy books about spells that I would do alone in the local woods, about all manner of things. Spells that would prosper me, bring me what I wanted and things that I felt I should have in my life. It was in that shop that I bought my first Tarot card deck, and my second. It was in that tiny shop where I gained an interest in crystals, runes and various divination modalities. The displays and the incense smell made everything feel appealing. It was an 'alternative' culture that I felt I should be a part of.

Around this time a Reiki healer came to 'heal' my stepdad from multiple sclerosis. He told me that I was already a 'healer' and that he could feel this from me, which tickled my ears and sparked my interest in crystal healing. I felt I was different from other people, that I was destined for great things, and my interest in the occult was what was going to unlock the world for me. I learnt the Tarot cards and runes, and I would tell my friends their fortune. Sometimes visions would be given to me and I would be amazed by their accuracy. I was being reeled in.

It was at university when I first heard, 'Jesus loves you!' being called out to me but I didn't give it a second thought. When I left university I joined a group of women who were teaching about crystals, divination and 'sensing' energies. It was a psychic circle, and that's where I learnt about my spirit guides. These spirits often lied, or led me down the wrong path, but I'd brush the 'mistakes' away as though the things that 'my guides' told just hadn't happened yet.

Leaving Home

I met a man through a temporary job when I was twenty, who I became infatuated with. I couldn't stop thinking about him, and decided that this was love. I was in my final year of university and my mum and stepdad were less than pleased at the situation, probably, and mostly, because he was fourteen years older than me. They tried to ban me from seeing him, which sent me further into his arms. There is nothing like strict rules and laying down the law to make a rebellious young adult run the other way. They both stopped talking to me when I decided to move into his bungalow for the summer holidays.

Even though it was a heart-wrenching time for me to be separated from my family and friends, I cast a spell so that we would stay together, and be bound to each other as I found comfort in him. The relationship was also an easy escape from the restrictions that were placed on me at my parental home. My spell was to keep us together, and I had certainty it would work. I didn't question 'who' was meeting my demands, I don't think I cared. It was proven to me that it worked when he proposed six months into our relationship. I will never fully know if he loved me – it never felt like he did. We couldn't have children despite having spent all of our wedding gift money on getting him a vasectomy reversal.

I had grown up in a Greek Orthodox family but pushed God to one side, although I don't remember why or when. However, we did get married in a Greek Orthodox church, which was expected of me. There was a lot to tie us together, but love was not forthcoming in the relationship for me, and my head was always being turned to work and anything else more interesting. Thirteen years later, we divorced and went our very separate ways.

Upgrading My False Spirituality

It was now 2006 and I met my current partner, who is a chef. Around this time the book *The Secret* by Rhonda Byrne came out, which was all about 'manifesting' what you want. This massively appealed to me and certainly many others. I read the book when it first came out, and by 2012 I was able to put some of my learnings into practice. It added to my 'witchy' interests.

My partner had told me early on he didn't approve of witchcraft and didn't want it around our children, but we both agreed that the 'universe' was giving us our desires, and that getting into a 'vibrational match' with the things we wanted (aka the occultic law of attraction), was okay. I got rid of some of my 'spell' books, but kept the ones that were better 'disguised'. I left most witchcraft to one side and went into what I saw as more 'sophisticated' forms of New Age practices, like 'manifesting' and 'goddess energy'.

I felt like with each new thing I was learning, I was 'levelling up' – there was always the next modality, and the next practice. That I was an ever-evolving goddess with the power to shape my reality. I considered doing a 'High Priestess' course, but always seemed to be pulled away from it. I attended many yoga lessons – classes for mums, classes for when you're pregnant, and loved it, it felt healthy. I went to a Kundalini awakening session once where the serpent energy is supposed to be awakened inside of you. I felt like I needed to go again and again as it felt like I was on the brink of a breakthrough with it.

I frequently used to go to 'women's circles', where at the start of a session we would call in our ancestors, dead spirits and energies of spirit beings we couldn't see. At the time it all felt like it was done with love, because I just didn't know what I was doing. The groups I would go to were very much pagan, with lots of shamanic practices mixed in with things like crystal healing. A soup of mix and match – all was good as long as it was 'good vibes', or working on my 'shadow'. You can just pick and mix the bits you like the most in the New Age as 'truths'.

All of my friends were into the same things as me, pretty much. We'd talk about what we were 'manifesting', in casual passing conversations, as though we were in charge and could align ourselves with the things we wanted. That all we had to do was to match the 'vibration' of the things we want to call into our lives. I looked down on people that were not on the same path to enlightenment. If something bad happened to us it was because on some level we had called it to ourselves, that *we* made it happen.

So we were all trying to 'flow better' with what we wanted from the 'universe', to 'raise our vibe' and push away things that didn't fit with our vision for our life. I only realise now how narcissistic that sounds. I was the 'god' in my life. And it was all about *me*. Self-development, self-enlightenment, self-love, self-realisation, self-actualisation, self, self, self.

I don't blame or look down on any of the people that are still doing these kinds of things, as I know that everyone is looking for love. Everyone who is spiritually seeking in the New Age is looking for the truth and wanting to better themselves. None of it is born out of hate. But the enemy seeks to tempt and deceive us. He looks to reel us into a different type of existence that keeps us asleep to many issues and away from God. Of course, at first, it's all shiny and lovely, until you go further on trying to 'level up'.

The Dream

Fast forward to 21st July 2023, and my partner and I were catering for an event as part of our catering business. The event was to mark the completion of a foraging course put together by a local charity, the Canal Trust. It was a gorgeous warm day, and my partner spent hours foraging wild flowers and herbs to go into the salad bowls he had put together. I complemented his finds by decorating the huge bowls of salad with mandalas, which brought a 'spiritual' vibe to them. I carefully placed petals in between leaves and sprigs and so on.

When we arrived he was asked to say a few things about the feast that we had just delivered. He talked about all the foraged leaves and flowers, and ended by thanking *God* for the abundance of food he had found. I was *shocked* and embarrassed, and, standing to one side, I felt my face blush.

When we got back into the car I complained about his speech, and in particular that people would think of him, and therefore us, as 'religious freaks'! I asked him not to do that again, and told him how embarrassed I was.

I had already decided that a recent friend was a 'nut job' for Jesus. My friend Lucinda had told me some months previously that she was now following Jesus. I did all I could to stop myself from asking, 'Where was he going?' in a sarcastic tone. Instead, I just nodded my head attentively and soon after clicked 'unfollow' on her Facebook profile. I felt like she had been fooled. She was now a boring Bible-basher type, and I thought it best to stay away. I'm sure she'll chuckle now reading that, especially since it was that very conversation that anchored me to her later down the line. If that conversation hadn't happened, I may have brushed off what was about to happen!

That very night, after the catering event, I had a dream. It was like no other dream I'd had before. It was so vivid and real and I now realise that it was full of symbology found in the Bible (which I hadn't read, and mostly ignored when picked up during Religious Education studies in school). In my dream, a group of us were sitting in a circle, roughly ten of us, and we were holding plates and eating, but it was raining. Directly above my head there was a loud bleating sound, like a sound of a trumpet. I looked around and asked everyone if they could hear it too. Before waiting for a response, I looked up and asked, 'Why are you making that noise?' As I said this, the clouds parted, and there were horses, a dove, and then finally

Jesus coming down from the sky in the brightest, brilliant white robe, with his hands held out – and I knew he was real.

Then, while still in the dream, everything suddenly went dark, and I knew it was judgement day. The streets were lined with people both dead and alive, waiting for their time to be judged. Directly in front of me was Princess Diana. She was with two other women. She was pacing and looked concerned, and they were talking to her gently. I reached over and touched her elbow, and told her that she had nothing to worry about. My mind went to my children, and I knew that they were with Jesus and that they were okay. And then a face that I can only describe as demonic was in front of my face, chattering, and talking at me in a language I did not understand. I found myself consumed in trying to understand what the face was telling me – and then it hit me . . . *Why am I wasting my time trying to figure it out when I could be looking at Jesus's face!* Then I woke up.

I suddenly realised that:

1. My children would be with Jesus and
2. I needed to prepare, and stop wasting my time.

Upon waking, I told my partner that 'Jesus is coming', and I started reading the Bible. I had several other dreams of Jesus too. It didn't just stop there – the same Jesus, the same face, the same feeling.

Church!

The day after my dream, I felt a pull to contact Lucinda. She put me in touch with 'The Bridge' and I asked my question in the Facebook group: 'Am I going crazy, or is this a real thing?' I also had a pull to go to church. When Lucinda told me that she went to the Baptist church in Stroud, which was directly opposite where my family and I used to live, I was sold on going. I already knew the street – I had been told 'Jesus loves me' on that very same street some years back. I already knew the minister – he greeted me in Greek the first time I met him so many years ago. I already knew some of the congregation because they gave us a piano! That house on that street was the house I lived in when I had joined Extinction Rebellion many years ago, and undertook various rebellious acts that saw me getting arrested – when I was told again that 'Jesus loves me'. Jigsaw pieces started to fall into place. As I look back across my life, Jesus had always been calling me home – he had always been there.

The first Sunday I walked into the church, the minister started crying. I didn't realise this was about me – but I wept too whilst my children hugged me. The songs that came on all seemed to point to my dream; they had lyrics included about trumpet sounds and keeping focused on Jesus's face. I realised I had been conned into the occult. It was all a lie.

Soon I realised that God wants a relationship with us. God wants an eternal relationship with us as his children. In the Bible, Paul tells us that 'God our Saviour . . . wants all people to be saved and to come to the knowledge of the truth' (1 Timothy 2:3-4). God has planned a way to make this relationship available to every human being, we simply need our hearts to soften enough to be able to start.

Jesus emphasises the power of even a small faith, using the analogy of a mustard seed, stating that with 'faith as small as a mustard seed' you can make mountains move (Matthew 17:20). The seed for me was planted. Thank you, God.

The week immediately after my first dream my five children and I got a stomach bug, and there was lots of vomiting and illness. At night, I could see dark shadows in my rooms and my dreams were agitated. One particular night I became very aware that there was a different realm that my soul existed in. I knew there was a battle happening for my soul, and that there were two sides. One side held me tight – there was no fighting, it was a steady, strong power. But the other side was the one that was battling, angry, agitated, and fighting for me (the gnashing of teeth comes to mind). My soul held onto Jesus. I woke up one night unable to breathe. On some level or realm that I was not physically part of, I knew if I called out to Jesus I'd be able to breathe again. It worked. At the end of the week, the battle was finished. My eldest daughter, who had immense trouble going to bed, let alone sleeping peacefully, suddenly stopped having nightmares, stopped having hysterics at bedtime, and now sleeps peacefully through the night. This was a miracle. Her nightmares had been a big pain point in my life, and it was all sorted!

In the first few weeks after the dream, I was looking for more confirmation. I needed more solid proof and looked in various places (mostly Google and the internet). There was a documentary that Lucinda shared with me that convicted me further. It was a five-hour documentary, and with a breastfeeding baby, I had to watch it in short snippets. Watching it in one go would have been too much for me to cope with. Suddenly, the veil fell from my eyes, and I could see the music and film industry, and secret societies, for what they were. It was horrific. I had a panic attack one evening because of the sheer evil that was revealed to me, and I realised that if whole industries are built around satanic worship – then Jesus is real, God is real, and all of this time I had been playing for the wrong team.

One morning after this, I was woken at about 5am by my breastfeeding toddler. As you do, I picked up my phone and started reading an article called 'Facts about the Bible', and within the article there was a YouTube video link that explained that there was a group of DNA experts that had found a piece of code in our DNA that seemed to carry a message. The message was in Aramaic, and was found to be a message from Yahweh, which is the Hebrew word for God. I couldn't believe it. I knew that searching the internet was going to give me mixed answers and that the only way to know for sure was to ask God himself.

I wept like a child, and prayed the hardest I have ever prayed with a fullness and purity of my heart, 'God, please show me *the truth.*' Was what I just read more lies or was it true? After being so deceived, I really needed to know the truth. I knew that we shouldn't test God, but I prayed that if this was true that Jesus would come to me in my dream right now. Against all odds, not only did I fall asleep at 7am – but I also had a dream! Guess who showed up . . .

A Second Dream

Now, this doesn't happen a lot – indeed, it hasn't happened since – that I sleep or snooze at this hour of the morning and have a dream within one hour. But this time was different. This time I *did* dream. Another dream like no other. It was Jesus *again.* His face was totally clear on a plant that belonged to my grandmother, and the plant was growing incredibly fast. I found this very funny in my dream, but when Jesus's face appeared on my plant, with a title written in gold lettering that said 'Bible Ministry', I was on the floor with amazement and *pure joy.* My Jesus, my Saviour, had answered and told me the truth. I needed confirmation, and there it was. I truly believe that when we ask God for us to be shown the answer, to have the truth revealed, and we ask this with an open heart, that he responds to us. The Bible says, 'Knock, and the door shall be opened to you' (Matthew 7:7).

In the Bible, Jesus told his disciples many times that he would be killed but he would come back to life on the third day. Yet, despite him telling them, and the Old Testament prophesying how this would all happen, his disciples were stunned to see Jesus was resurrected. And what did Jesus do when he found them? He asked for food, because they needed more proof. He tells them to look back at what has been said, because he knows that we need our *hearts* and *minds* to both believe, because when we have faith, both our hearts and our mind need to have faith. It was the same for me. With *all* glory to God, he put faith in my heart, and showed me the truth.

A month or so after my first dream, I felt like maybe I was going crazy, getting up early and going to church every Sunday. I prayed and asked God if I was going crazy. I said, 'I know we are not supposed to test you, God, but please can you give me an answer. Is this all real?' I picked up my Bible and opened it at a random page, or at least I thought it was a random page. To this day I cannot seem to be able to open my Bible to one of its shortest books, the book of Haggai, with just two chapters. The second chapter that I opened the Bible on starts with 'In the seventh month . . .' (I think to myself, July). It continues '. . . in the one and twentieth day of the month . . .' (I think 21st July) – Wait, what? 'came the *word of the Lord* . . .' I tried not to drop my Bible, but silently sat down on the edge of my bed. Astounded. What. Is. Going. On? Friends, readers – the 21st day of July was the day of my first dream! That's when the 'word of the Lord' first came to me. I used to be a gambler, too, and I would never have gambled on those odds happening. It is almost completely impossible.

I said, 'Thank you, Lord, I hear you. I'm going to church.' I thank God and praise him every day for how he speaks to me and shows me his ways. I may not hear him clearly in my ears, but he comes to me in my dreams. What a gift he has given me. I recently realised that the reason that he speaks to me through my dreams is that with five home-educated children in tow, that's the only time he can get my undivided attention at the moment.

Every week I go to church and the minister delivers messages directly from God, specifically for me. (It's not only for me, of course, but it really feels that way.) I'm sure that the only way that a human can say so many things that relate to the very questions and prayers I have been muddling through and uttering, is if God himself is involved. I may have been praying about my relationship; he'll preach about love. I may have been worrying about money or health; he'll preach about not worrying and having faith. I'd have questions or doubts about why I am bearing the load that I bear; he'll preach on endurance ... It happens *every week*. He reads from the Bible, and the Bible, God's Word, is my food. Indeed, the Bible says that

Jesus is the bread of life. My relationship with God has become utmost in my life.

Jesus has changed me, and every week he changes me more and sanctifies me, so gently and in his own way. I don't want to lead the life that I was leading before, of divination, witchcraft, goddess worship, self-idolatry, manifesting, worshipping creation and ignoring the Creator, chasing money, lying, cheating, even swearing, smoking cigarettes and weed, and sexual immorality. None of it even enters my head anymore and I actually feel repelled by those things. Instead, I find myself more patient, more in service, more loving, and a better mother and partner. When I have weeks that I am reading the Bible daily and praying with every opportunity, I am closer to God. And when I push my Bible time aside, I'm not as patient and loving. Jesus said, 'Abide in me, and I in you' (ESV). He wants me reading the Bible, he wants me to have a relationship with him.

All glory to God, he is the God of my life, not me. I want *his* will in my life, and his plans for me are better than those I have for myself. Every time I pray, he answers me. My faith lies in him alone, not all the misconceptions and lies that the world wanted me to buy into. I still fall way short of being like Jesus. Just because I became a Christian, it doesn't mean I became perfect overnight. But with the grace of God, the Holy Spirit guides me. He helps me to deal with life differently. The day I got baptised, the Holy Spirit filled me. It's was a feeling like no other, like a superpower where every cell in my body tingled. I just need to say 'Holy Spirit' even now, almost a year on, and he is there for me, and I am excited to see how I may serve him more.

I now know I am a child of God, Jesus is King and he will never forsake me. He is faithful and good and his love endures forever, always.

'Give thanks to the Lord, for he is good; his love endures forever.' (Psalm 107:1)

Laura's Story

Supernatural phenomena had fascinated me since childhood. My favourite cartoons and books were the ones featuring ghosts, and even at school, the first poem I ever wrote was about a ghost. My first short story was written for Halloween, unsurprisingly, and contained a ghostly theme. As a teenager, I loved movies and TV programmes featuring psychic and paranormal experiences, UFOs and the unexplainable.

My mother had psychic experiences and often shared accurate predictions. She had encountered visits from spirits and desired to further develop her abilities as a medium. She wanted to be able to speak with more of the spirit world, and was drawn into automatic writing and other New Age practices. While we were both out with my great-aunt one day, we all witnessed a UFO, adding to our intrigue and fascination with all things spiritual.

When I was around twelve years old my parents divorced. Soon after this my mum began visiting a local spiritualist church and her descriptions of what took place there enticed me to join her. Some months later, we both officially joined that church. Mediums apparently channelled 'spirit guides and spirits of the dead', relaying messages to the church congregation.

Cementing Our Beliefs

These 'spirit guides' or 'light beings' were extremely accurate and knew masses of information about people. They also shared predictions of the future and performed healings and other miracles. Like most mediums and channellers, the more we participated, the more our trust in these spirit beings grew.

Our spiritual worldview quickly began to match that of New Age teachings. We totally believed the spirit guides when they told us they were Ascended Masters, the ancient alien-gods from other star systems who had created life on earth. They said the Bible only held part-truths, and that Jesus was not the Saviour and heaven and hell didn't exist. Because the 'spirits of the dead' also said the same things, this further cemented our beliefs.

My mother's experience of automatic writing intrigued me, so as a teenager I was thrilled when mediums predicted I'd become a psychic artist when I was older. They said I would draw portraits and take infrared photographs of the deceased, as they 'appeared from the spirit world' for their enquiring family. Unknown to those mediums, my dad was an art teacher and I would go on to study art at college, so their predictions were plausible.

Whilst attending New Age fairs and workshops, we bought crystals and other recommended objects. We were keen to try alternative health remedies, self-help therapies and any courses aimed at our spiritual growth and enlightenment. Like many, we were also attracted to breathwork and things like mystical rebirthing classes. We were especially interested in learning how to 'raise our vibration', elevating our consciousness to become one with the 'source' and the 'universe'.

Astrology was a particular interest of mine and, due to the significance of the coming 'Great Awakening', or '(New) Age of Aquarius,' I felt proud to have Aquarius as my star sign. We found it funny that this zodiac sign was represented by the water-bearer, as swimming was one of my least favourite activities! As a teenager, I became addicted to a telephone service providing daily astrological readings. It became so expensive but I couldn't resist the allure of calling it. My mother eventually had to lock our family phone.

Although fascinating, we often felt there was still something missing, an almost tangible void within our souls that couldn't be satisfied. So, we were beguiled along the never-ending path of seeking more spiritual truths and experiences.

Our Situation Grew Dark

Most of the time we loved it and all seemed well for years, but sometimes we'd wonder if channelling spirits could actually be dangerous. Older mediums reassured us, telling us that mischievous or lower-level spirits coming through is a risk, and that psychic attacks *can* happen but most of the time only good spirits materialise. That they would teach us self-protection and spiritual warfare techniques. Was this good enough? Not truly convinced, but totally captivated, even addicted, like most spiritualists, we continued regardless.

Occasionally, concerning accounts circulated within the New Age community. Some mediums reported suffering serious difficulty; they were no longer able to channel spirits safely. That the spirits appeared against their will, becoming violent, forcing them into trances, even turning verbally, physically and sexually abusive. Some people were sharing that these spirits could become manipulative, lie or attempt to lead channellers astray.

Much to our horror, such experiences began happening to us. At home, spirits violently moved furniture or slammed doors. Electrical appliances began working even though they were disconnected from the power. Our cats and dogs were often alarmed by sudden movements, apparitions, or loud, unearthly noises. We were being physically attacked by entities and it felt truly hellish, like nothing we had experienced before.

Why would our spirit guides and dead relatives do this? They even physically threw my mum around! This greatly perplexed us. We couldn't really accept the explanations that the older mediums offered us. Some of them said it was a test sent from the spirit world. Others said these were signs of 'ascension symptoms' and should settle eventually. It felt like they didn't really know the answers and were trying to appease us.

Once, while outdoors, myself and others witnessed my mum being lifted and tossed over a car. Another time, while frying food, entities took control of her, forcing her into a trance, so that she became immobile and unaware as flames engulfed our kitchen. Thankfully, the local fire brigade arrived to extinguish it before it spread or destroyed our home. We were so relieved our pets had not been harmed.

We were often kept awake at night with intense supernatural phenomena, as evil forces terrorised us. We barely managed to function day to day, due to the chronic shock and trauma. Our relationships suffered, along with my school and then college work.

Searching For Answers

We visited our local library and researched paranormal and religious books, desperate for answers. We listed the names of numerous gods and entities, so that we could call out to them later, requesting their help. We believed that practising more meditation and yoga would help. Indeed, the other mediums recommended this, assuring us this would connect us with 'higher guides', who would evict negative spirits and therefore help us ascend out of the darkness.

As with Reiki, practices like meditation and yoga are commonplace today. Most don't realise that these can yoke you with spirits, even if you do not sense them. Indeed, if you research their origins, this is their primary function, to deliberately open you to the spirit world and for the worship of various gods. These practices were not taught throughout Eastern philosophies for mere gentle relaxation, as many assume. Original yogis, New Agers, witches and occultists have acknowledged this for centuries, and so these were naturally considered to be of great significance in our spiritual journey.

We questioned why the unwelcome paranormal activity grew worse. Sometimes, the spirits even spoke with our voices, or voices of other living people, not just ghostly voices. We slowly started to wonder if all spiritual entities could be imposters. Could any cosmic being help us survive this battle? We reached the end of our tether.

This continued for years. While studying art at college, I met the kind young man who later became my dear husband. Setting up our own apartment was exciting but when I was moving from my parental home, I was reluctant to leave my mother alone with the spirits. My husband and I were delighted when our precious baby boy came into the world. However, spirits continued to attack me. Some of them clearly followed me from my mum's home, taking up residence in our apartment.

None of our beloved channeller friends or spiritualist churches within the New Age community could help. Sadly, they deserted us. We heard of others undergoing such rejection too.

My mother requested sleeping pills from her doctor due to the regular night-time harassment but he didn't believe her story. Tragically, like many other occultists, my mum was diagnosed as schizophrenic. To our shock, she was detained in a psychiatric hospital. Along with our family, I was heartbroken. We remembered hearing of this sadly happening to some other spirit mediums.

Those early days of visiting my mother became a blur. Seeing her in that psychiatric ward, amongst so much suffering, I became frozen in a state of agony and unbelief. Due to the powerful drugs she was being prescribed, she would move in an almost robotic, zombie-like manner, shuffling around very slowly and mechanically. As a result, she felt humiliated and broken. I wanted more than anything for her to be free. It felt as if I had lost my mother and I longed to have her back again.

He Stands At the Door and Knocks

Then, while studying for a psychology degree at university, I was befriended by Susan, a Christian. She claimed that Jesus could help our situation. Presuming she was spiritually unevolved and far from enlightened, I listened – albeit reluctantly. After all, I knew spirit mediums who apparently channelled Jesus, saying he was merely an Ascended Master.

Susan said a Christian minister with the prophetic gift would soon be speaking at a nearby church during Easter weekend. Being a New Ager, and fascinated by predictions, I decided to go along.

It was unlike any Christian church service I'd attended before, whether at Christmas or for the occasional wedding. Those churches had all seemed irrelevant, dull and boring, with no power of God evident, no miracles or changed lives. But in comparison, this particular Christian church was different, with a lively atmosphere and engaging sermon. I loved it. It deeply impressed me. More importantly, a strong spiritual *presence* I hadn't encountered before overwhelmed me. I was convinced this was the peak spiritual experience of my life so far. It felt like liquid love, exquisitely beautiful and peaceful. I was totally intrigued by this 'spirit being', or God, as it felt unlike any I'd ever met before and left me thirsting for more information.

People sang and prayed in other tongues. This fascinated me. Their prayers for healing intrigued me too.

Something supernatural was clearly occurring, yet they weren't channelling spirits. I could imagine enjoying going there every Sunday and attending midweek meetings too. I really could not wait to go again! Whilst travelling home, multiple questions raced through my mind.

It was astonishing to find the spirits and spirit guides, including our dead relatives, were clearly furious I'd visited that church. Returning home was utterly horrendous. Knowing that mum's spirit guides had led to her incarceration, I knew that mine intended to destroy me that night. They were enraged that I was heading out of the occult, towards the Lord. They wanted me dead. I sensed it. They dreaded our experiences being shared to awaken others.

Although I didn't invite Jesus into my life that particular night, he began to consume my mind. Desperately, I wondered if he truly is the Saviour. So I prayed, asking him to show me if he was real. That very same night, when those beings reappeared again, I shouted the name of Jesus Christ at them and they vanished. The supernatural attacks stopped!

This astounded me. Absolutely nothing we tried before had succeeded. I was deeply grateful and I felt Jesus had just saved my life. After years of spiritual torture, surely peace would now finally enter and reign in my life? I was still unsure about Jesus being the Saviour but, as a truth-seeker, I was keen to find out. However, at the same time, it was extremely unnerving to realise everything spiritual I'd been taught and believed in was probably lies. I didn't actually want to believe this and felt a tug-of-war within my mind, as cognitive dissonance reached its height.

That night, drifting asleep, it puzzled me why I kept remembering a fortune-teller who sometimes visited our neighbourhood.

The next morning our doorbell rang. To my great surprise, it was her! Rather than offering a palm-reading as usual, she blurted out, 'I've become a Christian. Jesus freed me from spirits and psychic powers. He brought me here today to tell you that the place you visited last night has *the truth.*'

> 'He reached down from on high and took hold of me; he drew me out of deep waters. He rescued me from my powerful enemy, from my foes, who were too strong for me.' (Psalm 18:16-17)

In my heart, I felt confirmation had arrived. All the jigsaw pieces were finally falling into place. The last thing I had imagined was becoming a Christian, it never appealed to me, yet as a truth-seeker I could not deny where the evidence led.

True Clarity

It felt as if a veil was suddenly swept from my eyes and I was struck by a divine revelation that Jesus is real. I just knew this was the truth! This changed everything. The world was not as it seemed. There really is a God and he was reaching out to me! I realised that there are not *many* paths to God – Jesus is the *only way!* I couldn't wait to tell my mother at our next visit but she was doubtful, having been so steeped in New Age ideologies.

I realised I'd been so open minded as a New Ager, willing to accept a range of spiritual beliefs and practices. So, why not Jesus? I asked myself. I thought to myself that if he is the truth, then this is critically important to truly *know*.

'Jesus answered, "I am the way and the truth and the life. No one comes to the Father except through me."' (John 14:6)

I soon asked Jesus Christ to become my Saviour. I felt extremely thankful to start developing a personal, lifelong relationship with him. I asked him to forgive me from all of my sin, both in thought and action. I renounced everything, rejecting New Age, Spiritualism, and anything involving other religions and spiritualities, witchcraft or the occult.

It seemed so beautiful to me that I received Christ during Easter. Just as the church celebrated his atonement for us and resurrection from the dead, I was rising from spiritual death and embarking in a new life with him. This was incredibly humbling. It felt embarrassing, remembering the spiritual pride I held as a New Ager, feeling chosen and superior to everyone else, on my alleged journey of enlightenment.

Upon joining my friend's church, I was thrilled to hear of apologetics, an academic discipline. Contrary to popular belief, not all academia disproves Christianity. Many worldwide scholars, including university professors, teaching archaeology, history and the sciences, provide evidence for biblical authenticity and the existence of biblical figures, including Jesus. He is not a mythical figure, or a 'reincarnation' of ancient 'saviour-gods'. He is the son of God and alive right now!

It amazed me that evidence exists proving biblical records are factual, especially regarding Jesus. Most historians admit there is sufficient evidence to support that Jesus did live, die on a cross, and rise again – just as the Bible describes. Plus, despite New Age teachings, there is absolutely no proof any other 'god' in history died for our sins, nor rose again.

I felt utterly desperate to help my mother. I felt sure she'd agree with these findings and so I looked forward to my next visit with her in the hospital.

While I was beginning to read the Bible, I would sense God answering my questions. Thinking, or praying over issues, I'd discover explanations. It's amazing talking to our Creator instead of spirits. Why seek knowledge from divination, or other similarly demonic sources, rather than directly from God himself?!

'There shall not be found among you any one ...
that useth divination, or an observer of times, or an
enchanter, or a witch. Or a charmer, or a consulter
with familiar spirits, or a wizard, or a necromancer
... these things are an abomination unto the Lord.'
(Deuteronomy 18:10-12 KJV)

'And no wonder, for Satan himself masquerades
as an angel of light. It is not surprising ...
his servants also masquerade as servants of
righteousness.' (2 Corinthians 11:14-15)

Pretending to kindly offer guidance for years, these
evil masters of disguise had baited and betrayed
us. My spiritual worldview now began to align with
scripture. Reading the Bible 'renewed my mind'.
It felt like an epiphany of a lifetime as I suddenly
stopped believing in the existence of ghosts, spirit
guides, other gods and alien UFOs. I now believed
the biblical explanation that they are all evil demons,
masquerading as if they are other beings. That their
main aim is to deceive humankind, especially about
the origins of life on earth, and the truth about Jesus,
heaven and hell.

Therefore, it made perfect sense to me that Ascended
Masters and ghosts don't exist, and the reason they
all lie about the afterlife is to lead us away from faith
in Jesus, or to stop us from seeking his forgiveness.
I now understood reincarnation was impossible
and that experiences of past-life regressions were
deceptive, caused by demons evoking false memories.

It now appeared logical that reports of meeting 'alien-gods' during 'astral projections' were also counterfeit experiences. I realised it's easy for demons to shape-shift into other beings, or produce alleged advanced technology and aircraft, bringing forth false depictions of UFOs.

I now saw the spiritual darkness behind the New Age false light, and that within my beloved Age of Aquarius, all that glitters is definitely not gold. So, at the advice of my friend's church and my own desire, I burned my New Age and spiritualist material. Throughout the Bible, when people repented for such beliefs, they burned their books and paraphernalia, severing occult ties, thereby making a clean start with God.

My Mum

I shared everything I had discovered with my mother, and although she was sceptical at first, it wasn't long before she admitted that she was not surprised. Much to my sheer delight, she then asked to attend church with me. The hospital allowed me to take her out, and after just a few visits to church and hearing about Jesus, my mother, a 'spirit medium', asked Jesus to become her Saviour! She repented of her sins and the occult, and also destroyed all her related paraphernalia. We were overjoyed!

Her mood lifted and she stopped talking about spirits to the psychiatric team. We soon saw a huge improvement in her. Her doctors clearly noticed and, to our great joy, my mum was released from the hospital.

However, once back home, her torment started again. This didn't surprise us, as the spirits had not yet been evicted. Our pastor, having never cast out demons before, assumed that now we were Christians, there could no longer be any demons around. But they still harassed her as well as me, too, in the home I shared with my beloved husband and our young child.

Suddenly, a tragic catastrophe struck. One summer's morning, just a few short months after my conversion, an envelope arrived. Immediately, I recognised my mum's handwriting. The contents were unthinkable. I opened it to discover a suicide letter from my mother. I heard a loud, ear-piercing scream, then realised it was my own. To my utter shock and dismay, my mum had tragically committed suicide.

My own dear mother had taken her life with an overdose of sleeping pills. She had lost all hope and the ongoing torment and misery proved too much for her. I was completely devastated. Not only was her suicide totally heart-breaking for me, I feared this disastrous outcome could also happen to me. It felt as if my life was racing downhill fast. My mother had literally killed herself. I can't possibly even begin to describe how I felt.

As I had only received Christ three months earlier, I was still a baby Christian, still learning. Back then, I realised there might be other churches that could help us, but I had actually thought that my pastor would soon discern the truth and deliver my mother and me from demons. I didn't think we'd need to look beyond that church for help. I had assured my mum that Jesus would help, after all, we both knew he cast out demons in the Bible. I thought she believed the pastor would soon come and solve our situation. Maybe she didn't want to dampen my enthusiasm by admitting she doubted anyone would help.

Whilst grieving I wondered if, had I actually been successful at persuading our pastor to help, it could have saved my mother's life. As a result, like many affected by suicide, I suffered deeply from guilt and regret.

At that time, as a new believer, I didn't realise that any Christian experienced at casting demons out could have helped my mum. Little did I know then that a couple of years later, even though I didn't seek after the deliverance ministry, that the Lord would graciously equip me to help others by casting out demons.

I am convinced if the church had evicted the demons tormenting my mother that she would still be alive today. I've heard countless similar tragedies since her suicide, in 1996. This highlights why it is crucial that churches cast demons out, just as Jesus and his disciples did.

Freedom and Walking in New Life

Not only had demons preyed on my mother, my own suffering continued. I had repented and destroyed my occult books, but demons continued to terrorise me. I wondered how long I'd remain their victim. Every now and then, they'd attack me and pin me down. Spluttering and choking, I'd try to move but heavy weights crushed my chest and invisible hands strangled me. Intense evil presences surrounded me. Trying to pray, I'd be paralysed and couldn't speak. Struggling, I'd eventually manage to shout Christ's name and the demons would leave. But I received only temporary relief, until the next time.

Unknown to me then, these are classic examples of demonic attack as reported by Christians and others. Thankfully, it finally ends upon intentionally seeking full deliverance, from Jesus, as I soon gratefully discovered for myself.

Just as demons had driven my mother to suicide, I knew they also wanted my death, to silence my voice, preventing my testimony from alerting others to the truth.

I went to my pastor again. He still insisted Christians couldn't have demons in their homes or bodies. Like many, he assumed the moment you receive Christ into your life, demons automatically leave, without being deliberately cast out.

Not believing demonic deliverance was required, and knowing of my mother's incarceration and subsequent suicide, the pastor advised my husband to incarcerate me in a psychiatric hospital. Thankfully, my dear husband appreciated this was a spiritual issue, rather than my mental health.

Seeking a helpful church involved a long, frustrating search for me and my husband. Eventually, we found one that could help us. One day, while listening to Christian radio, a minister shared the testimonies of all the people he had helped over fifty years, casting demons from them. His church was in our city!

The disciples prayed for diseases to be healed, and cast demons out from anyone requiring deliverance. They never specified it is only unbelievers who need physical healing, or demonic liberation. God warned believers throughout scripture to avoid witchcraft and false gods because he knows they cause defilement by evil spirits. 'Regard not them that have familiar spirits, neither seek after wizards, to be defiled by them: I am the Lord, your God' (Leviticus 19:31 KJV).

I visited, then quickly joined the church of the pastor I'd heard on the radio. Casting demons from me and our home, their ministers used no rituals, religious icons or paraphernalia. Just faith and authority in the name, cross and blood of Jesus Christ, was enough to evict them. Demons were also banished from my late mother's home and we sold it with a clear conscience, trusting new tenants would not be harassed.

Most people aren't surprised at demons being cast out of former demon worshippers, or Satanists. That I needed deliverance from demons, as a former spiritualist, should not be a surprise either. The apostle Paul cast a demon from a psychic:

'We were met by a female slave who had a spirit by which she predicted the future. She earned a great deal of money for her owners by fortune-telling ... Paul ... said to the spirit, "In the name of Jesus Christ I command you to come out of her!" At that moment the spirit left her.' (Acts 16:16, 18).

Jesus continued to heal my past. Sometimes during worship, in church or at home, I'd begin crying. A refreshing inner-release or purging would occur, which was not upsetting or unpleasant. My focus was overcome by the love, beauty and majesty of the Lord, not the purging itself. Afterwards, I'd feel lighter, as if weights had lifted from my shoulders.

After my new pastor cast demons from me and our home in 1996, there were no more visits from so-called ghosts, or Ascended Masters. It never happened again. No demon appeared masquerading as my dead mother either.

Since then, I've heard countless testimonies from Christians worldwide who also struggled to find a helpful church. Many, like my mum, entered psychiatric hospitals, or became suicidal. Tragically, some did commit suicide, with their loved ones sharing their stories.

My entire life and mindset changed. Christ continued to lift layers of deception and trauma from me. As a new Christian, the scripture, 'You will not fear the terror of night' (Psalm 91:5) brought great encouragement. I felt God's assurance that I would no longer be attacked by ghostly figures, especially during the night hours.

Since 1996, not once have demons contacted me, masquerading as ghosts or spirit guides, and all dreams of 'alien visitations' ended. Knowing that I am aware of their true identity, they never attempt to trick me with shape-shifting appearances, or diabolical spiritual lies anymore.

Instead of fearing demons, Jesus enabled me to overcome, then to free others and their homes, of demons, by the power of his name. He radically changed and emboldened me. We can minister to others, if anointed with Christ's love and power, ushering them to faith and freedom, even those saved from the darkest sins or occult lifestyles.

'He has delivered us from the dominion of darkness . . . in whom we have redemption, the forgiveness of sins.' (Colossians 1:13-14)

Jesus achieved a work of transformation in my life. Once imprisoned in a demonic dungeon, he smashed the chains, setting me free.

'The cords of death entangled me, torrents of destruction overwhelmed me ... in my distress I called to the Lord ... From his temple he heard my voice.' (Psalm 18:4-6)

I'm so relieved my endless seeking of new truths and experiences from the New Age is over. Their predictions of me becoming a medium specialising in psychic art and photography never came true.

Jesus is what my mum and I had always felt was missing. Like other believers, I am far from perfect and remain a work in progress as the Holy Spirit continues the process of changing and refining me. Although life will always be challenging in this world, the Holy Spirit lovingly walks with us, guiding us through it.

Since 2009, I have been honoured to serve through ministry and to speak at events, weekend conferences and so on. My work is shared throughout Christian, secular and even New Age media. Precious people contact me requesting advice, or to share their similar testimonies with me. Thank you for reading my testimony. I pray the Lord uses it to bring you his hope and encouragement. May God bless you.

So What Comes Next?

You have read ten stories from people who have
bared their souls. These testimonies are a drop in the
ocean compared to what God is doing in the New
Age around the world right now. Many of the authors
already knew the spirit realm was real but had no
idea they were in a battle, let alone that they had got
caught up on the wrong side. They have shared all
about the darkness and spiritual wickedness they were
involved in, and how chasing spiritual highs, or even
just desiring peace and to heal from feeling broken in
some way, had far-reaching consequences.

There are thousands more similar testimonies being
lived out right now. God is at work in the New Age,
pulling his sons and daughters out of the darkness
and into his light, the only true light.

People are discovering that what they were always
searching for was God, that the hole in their soul
was 'God shaped'. Some of the testimonies in these
pages are extreme because of the spiritual doorways

opened, but there are many more less dramatic stories of meeting God. There is no right or wrong way, only God's way in God's timing. He knows us all intimately and knows when and how to reach out to us.

He may be wanting to reach out to you right now through this very book. Have you been wrestling with your thoughts about whether you can truly trust that God is real? Have you wondered if he really does desire a relationship with you? Do you feel the walls of the spiritual worldview you had created are tumbling down? Are you thinking to yourself, 'Could I have got it wrong all this time?' Please know that he is offering out his hand to you right now. He is offering you the free gift of forgiveness and eternal life through his Son, Jesus Christ.

We all fall short of God's holy standard, and in his mercy and love he made a way for us to get into a right relationship with him. That *way* is through Jesus. Like Jesus says in the Bible, 'I am the way and the truth and the life. No one comes to the Father except through me' (John 14:6). The *way* is Jesus and believing in what he did for you on the cross 2,000 years ago. Knowing that he gave his life so that 'whosoever believes in him shall not perish but have eternal life' (John 3:16). So whatever spiritual path you have been on, whatever darkness masquerading as light you have been following, it is not too late to turn away from the counterfeit and follow the one true God. The God who made you and who knitted you together in your mother's womb. He loves you and is calling you home.

Some of us encounter Jesus and take an immediate about-turn to follow him with the help of the Holy Spirit, but for many it can be a slower journey. This can take time and diligently looking into evidence for Jesus' life, death and resurrection. If this is you then there are resources we can recommend (listed at the end of this book) to help with your search. If you would like to, here is a prayer you can say:

'Jesus, if you are real, would you please reveal yourself to me? If you really are the truth then I do want to follow you and get to know you and have a relationship with you. Please help me to find you. Amen.'

If you feel ready right now to accept God, through Jesus, into your heart, then this next prayer is for you.

'Father God, I am sorry I went my own way and for all the things I have done that missed your mark. Thank you for reaching out to me through your Son, Jesus Christ. Thank you for what you did for me at the cross, that you died for me and that you rose again. Please cleanse me and please forgive my sins. Thank you. I receive you into my life as Lord and Saviour. Please help me to turn from my ways to follow your way. Thank you, Father God. Thank you, Lord Jesus. Thank you, Holy Spirit. I pray these words in the holy and precious name of Jesus, amen.'

If you have just said this prayer from the bottom of your heart, welcome home! You have just taken the first step into a new life of freedom, peace and joy. It does not mean life will suddenly be all sunshine and roses. We live in this fallen world, and life will be challenging. If you have been deep in occultic New Age practices, you may be entering a battle for a period of time as the devil does not want to lose you. But you have a King in Christ who has already conquered all powers of darkness at the cross and you can walk in that knowledge and faith.

We are meant to walk the path of following Jesus in a community of other believers, so if you have just taken the wonderful first step on this journey, find a local Bible-believing, Spirit-filled church. You may need to try a few, and pray for God to let you know where he wants you to settle and grow your faith. If you want further support, The Bridge is here for you. You can join the Facebook community by searching 'The Bridge (New Age to Jesus)' where you are welcome to ask any questions you may have and to meet others who have walked a similar path out of the New Age to follow Jesus.

God bless your seeking and searching,

'Then you will know the truth, and the truth will set you free.' (John 8:32)

'This is the message we have heard from him and declare to you: God is light; in him there is no darkness at all.' (1 John 1:5)

Glossary

Note: Because the New Age is so wide and varied, definitions may vary depending on who is defining the concepts.

3D – the physical reality. This is a newer belief that has its roots in Gnosticism and is that existing in the physical reality is a lower state of consciousness.

5D – it is believed that through the ascension process humans can raise their vibration to exist at a higher state of consciousness where they live in a state of pure love and unconditional acceptance.

Age of Aquarius – a new astrological era, predicting a golden age to come, whereby humanity raises its consciousness and lives in unity. A great proponent and promoter of the theory was Helena Blavatsky. It is where the term 'New Age' came from.

Akashic Records – a supposed spiritual record of every thought and action of every soul that has taken place in the universe.

Amulet – a small object or piece of jewellery thought to offer protection from danger or evil spirits.

Arcturian – (see starseed) extra terrestrial beings from the Arcturian star cluster.

Ascended Masters – beings who achieved enlightenment within one lifetime, such as the Buddha and Jesus. In the New Age, Jesus is not the Son of God, but just a normal human who managed to achieve enlightenment.

Ascension – the belief that we can ascend to a 'higher level of consciousness'.

Ascension Symptoms – generally negative and temporary. Physical, mental or emotional changes that take place as a result of a spiritual 'leap' or 'breakthrough'.

Ashram – a generally Hindu spiritual hermitage or monastery where people stay for differing periods of time. Often worship of a 'guru' is the focus of spiritual life.

Astral Projection – an out of body experience, perceived as the separation of a person's consciousness from their body. It is said by those who practise astral projection that they are able to travel around spiritual planes/realms.

Ayahuasca – a plant with psychedelic properties which is brewed in a tea. It is used for shamanic journeys to enable communication with spirits and to reach a higher state of consciousness.

Blood Magic – a specific form of witchcraft that draws power from blood. In the New Age it is commonly connected to goddess, earth worship and general female empowerment work using menstrual blood.

Body Code and the Emotion Code – these are spiritual practices created by Bradley Nelson, based on the belief that the body can heal itself. It's a way of tapping into the unconscious mind to 'release energy blockages' in the body to improve physical, mental and spiritual well-being.

Breathwork – different forms of controlled breathing to promote relaxation, improve physical and mental health, and healing.

Chakras – these are believed to be spinning energy centres in the body. Various different spiritual practices are thought to help the health of chakras to ensure energy flow through the 'root' chakra, up to the 'crown' chakra.

Channelling – the process of communicating with spirit guides, Ascended Masters or beings from other planets to receive spiritual information (in reality they are demons). Can also be used to describe the process of letting a spirit fully take over and use the human as a vessel to speak.

Christ Consciousness – the idea that we all have a spark of the divine in us, that we are all gods like Christ.

Darkness Therapy – spending time in a pitch-dark room for an extended period for healing and spiritual growth.

Divine Feminine Energy – an energetic force that flows within people that is characterised by empathy, intuition and strong connections to others and to the earth.

DMT – a strong psychedelic drug that affects consciousness and perception.

DMT Machine Elves – spirit beings frequently reported to be seen by people when they take DMT. A term first coined by Terence McKenna who was famous for psychedelic use and experimentation.

Eastern Mysticism – a broad term to describe mystical traditions coming from Eastern religions.

Energy Medicine – is believed to be a way of healing energy imbalances in the body to improve physical and mental health, and to promote spiritual advancement. It can take many different forms such as Reiki, acupuncture, crystal healing, or Theta healing.

Frequency/Vibration – the idea that we can change the vibrating frequency of items, people, places and thoughts through spiritual practices that are thought to raise our 'vibration'. This is connected to believing in 'ascension' in terms of spiritual enlightenment and consciousness.

Gnosticism – religious and spiritual ideas emphasising that secret knowledge is the way to salvation. Gnosticism emerged during the era of the early church and now is woven into New Age ideas. Often includes a belief that the God of the Old Testament is evil and controlling.

Goddess Work – often centred around goddess temples. Courses where people train to become goddess 'High Priestesses'. Connected to earth worship and paganism.

Hermeticism – this philosophy comes from the writings of Hermes Trismegistus who received 'spiritual wisdom' about medicine, law, art, music, philosophy and magic whilst in a trance. The ancient Egyptians called him a 'voice of the gods'.

Higher Self – a concept that describes a higher spiritual aspect of oneself. Often seen in connection to a Higher Power.

Human Design – this is a complex system that combines Western astrology, Chinese I Ching and Judaic Kabbalah, with pseudoscientific interpretations of quantum mechanics, in order to understand more about the self. The system was created by a man called Ra Uru Hu, who channelled the information from a being (demon) who he referred to as 'the voice'.

Kambo – a South American healing ritual that involves the poisonous venom from a frog.

Kundalini – this is believed to be a form of energy that lies dormant, coiled up like a snake at the base of the spine and awakened through various practices such as Kundalini yoga, Tantra and more.

Law of Attraction – this is the concept that 'like attracts like'; that if we think positive thoughts and visualise and 'vibrate' at the same frequency of what we want, that we will attract it in reality. We can 'manifest' our own chosen reality.

Lightworkers – it is believed that these are 'awakened' people who are operating at a higher state of consciousness, and are here to assist humanity to raise their vibration.

Luciferianism – Lucifer and Satan are the same being in the Bible. Those who worship him as Lucifer believe that he is a god of light, knowledge and magic.

Manifestation – this is basically the 'law of attraction', the idea that everything that happens to us is something we've created with our thoughts and feelings. So it's believed if we cultivate positive thoughts, feelings and visualise positive things, then good things will happen to us.

Multi-faith Ministers – the training and professional practice of becoming a 'Reverend' to support people of all faiths or none with ceremonies and the like.

Mystery Schools – it is believed that these schools taught ancient occult knowledge, and practices such as meditation and astral projection. In these schools, people study the self and they are founded on the belief that we are all divine beings. It is believed that behind all religions and philosophies in the world are these mystery school teachings which are the root of truth.

New Age – the term New Age comes directly from occult teaching about the new spiritual age to come. The words 'New Age' were taken from the (new) *Age of Aquarius,* or in more recent times this has more often been referred to as *the great awakening.* The New Age is an umbrella term that encompasses many different spiritual practices. It could be described as a 'spiritual' smorgasbord where people can pick different flavours of spiritual practice. This means there are unlimited ways of being a New Ager, although people under the New Age umbrella rarely identify with the term as either a wider description or a personal label. The New Age is essentially a counterfeit of God's kingdom.

New Thought – belief that we can gain mastery and control of our lives through positive thoughts and beliefs.

Obsidian Mirror Work – it is believed that obsidian crystals can be a mirror to the soul, revealing people's 'light' and 'shadow' sides. An obsidian mirror is used as a way to meditate and connect with one's 'higher self'.

Ouija Board – a tool used to communicate with spirits, consisting of letters on a board and a glass that moves around the board and spells out words.

Past-life Regression – a specific type of hypnotherapy thought to help people access and explore past lives, based on the belief of reincarnation.

Pellowah – a 'hands off' form of energy healing similar to Reiki, thought to be more 'spiritual'.

Pendulum – an item, often made from crystal, that hangs on a string or chain. It is used for divination.

Plant Medicine Ceremonies – (also see shamanism), these are shamanic ceremonies using different psychedelic plants, such as ayahuasca, iboga, some kinds of mushrooms.

Pleiadian – (see starseed), extra-terrestrial beings from the Pleiadian star cluster.

Polarity Teachings – the idea that each human is made up of masculine and feminine energy. There are different modalities that either focus on balancing them within ourselves, or by becoming more feminine or masculine depending on our gender, we can advance spiritually, achieve happiness and improve relationships.

Quantum Healing Hypnosis – A method created by Dolores Cannon that claims to regress people to their past lives for healing.

Rebirthing – a practice that can be varied. Sometimes including breathwork. Often focused on healing trauma from birth and early childhood, or more general spiritual healing or ascension.

Reflexology – a system of massage to relieve tension and treat illness, based on the idea that there are reflex points in the body that can become blocked and inhibit the flow of 'chi/qi' which is believed to be the 'life-force' in Taoism.

Reiki – a healing technique based on the idea that spiritual energy can be channelled into a person to improve physical or mental health. Usually done in person, sometimes as hands-on healing.

Reincarnation – the belief that people live more than one life.

Self-realisation – in Eastern traditions it can be thought of as achieving a higher spiritual state of understanding oneself as part of something greater, aka the 'universe'.

Shadow Work – this comes from the work of Carl Jung and it is the concept that we can bring the darker 'repressed' parts of ourselves into the light, and learn to love and accept them.

Shakti – is a Hindu goddess who is used in the New Age to represent the 'divine feminine energy'.

Shamanism – shamans use singing, dance, movement and plant medicine to achieve altered states of consciousness to connect with the 'spirit world'.

Singing Bowl Healing – (see Sound Healing)

Sound Healing – using different sounds such as gongs, tuning forks, shamanic drumming and crystal singing bowls to promote relaxation and enter a trance-like state. It is believed that the vibrations of the music can promote healing and spiritual transformation. Often offered in combination with a shamanic-style visualisation 'journey' meditation.

Spirit Medium – a psychic who can supposedly communicate with the spirits of dead loved ones, who are actually demons masquerading as other kinds of spirits.

Starseeds – 'special souls' who have previously lived on other planets who incarnate on earth to help humanity ascend to a higher state of consciousness.

Sweat Lodge – a heated hut used for shamanic purification ceremonies in many indigenous cultures. It is believed that the shape of the lodge represents the womb of mother earth so people can return to their creator for healing and spiritual advancement.

Tai Chi – originally a martial art from China that developed into a form of moving meditation.

Taoism – an ancient Chinese philosophy based on the idea that there is a cosmic force, 'chi', which flows through all things.

Tantra – a spiritual practice that combines sexuality with meditative practice. It originates from Hindu and Buddhist texts but has evolved into more Westernised spiritual practices.

Tarot – a form of divination using a special pack of seventy-eight pictorial cards.

Theosophy – an occult religious movement founded by Helena Blavatsky, a spirit medium who channelled information for her books.

Transcendental Meditation – a form of meditation where people quietly repeat a mantra to enter a state of relaxation.

Twin Flame – a New Age concept where one soul is said to have been split into two separate bodies.

Universe – in the New Age the 'universe' is used as a counterfeit of God. It's a cosmic unity where everything exists, and it is conscious.

Resources

New Age Deception

The Second Coming of the New Age: The Hidden Dangers of Alternative Spirituality in Contemporary America and Its Churches – by Josh Peck and Steven Bancarz. (Steven also has content on a YouTube channel.)

The Hidden Dangers of the Rainbow – by Constance Cumbey.

Happy Lies – by Melissa Dougherty.

Confronting the New Age: How to Resist a Growing Religious Movement – by Douglas Groothuis.

Evidence for Jesus's Life, Death and Resurrection

A Case for Christ – by Lee Strobel. (Also a movie.)

Evidence That Demands a Verdict: Life-changing Truth for a Sceptical World – by Sean McDowell and Josh McDowell.

Christian Apologetics: An Introduction – by Alister McGrath.

Biblical Archaeology: A Very Short Introduction – by Eric H. Cline.

More New Age to Jesus Testimonies

Starseed to Jesus – by Sarah-Jayne Lee.

Witchcraft to Christ – by Doreen Irving. (You can also find her teaching videos on YouTube.)

Authentic Awakening – by Alan Strudwick.

The Beautiful Side of Evil – by Johanna Michaelson.

Brahmin Reborn – by Bhaskar Sreerangam.

Yeshua Testimonies (YouTube channel).

There are also hundreds, if not thousands, of personal New Age to Jesus testimonies on YouTube.

Discipleship

The Bible! – it is helpful to start by reading about Jesus's life, ministry, death and resurrection in one of the gospels. The book of John is an accessible place to start.

Bibleforlife.co.uk

Bibleproject.com

Other

The Bridge (New Age to Jesus) – Facebook group

Thebridgeministry.org.uk

www.ingramcontent.com/pod-product-compliance
Lightning Source LLC
Chambersburg PA
CBHW062057080426

42734CB00012B/2681